WHO'S RIGHT?

WHO'S WRONG?

BY   TOM NORTON

DEDICATED

TO THOSE WHO WOULD RATHER WRITE
A BOOK THAN READ ONE.

TABLE OF CONTENTS

As this book's content consists of well over one hundred numbered topics, page numbers will not be necessary. As they are short topics and numbered, any topic or location can be quickly located by thumbing through the book and utilizing the numbers of other topics. The topics are numbered as follows.

Who's right and who's wrong?

Well, you can be the judge of that.

INTRODUCTION

The point of writing the book is that the author knows that everyone perceives things in a different way and no one will be in agreement with the perceptions in the book. Why our perceptions are different is the question.

About half of everything that each individual, including myself, believes to be factual is erroneous. There are many reasons for this and if this was not the case, everyone on Earth would be in agreement of everything. If the reader is correct in all of his beliefs, then he is the only one in six billion people. How can six billion people be wrong and you be right?

As you read this book you may quickly get the impression or perceive that I am the most cynical person in the world. It appears that I find something wrong with everything in the world, past and present. Well, of course I do, as there *is* something wrong with everything in the world. Any Evolutionist will tell you that is why everything evolves, in order to better itself. Creationists will also tell you that there is something wrong with all of us and that is why we must be so vigilant in our worship and the constant teaching of the scriptures. All manufacturers will admit that there was something wrong with last year's model and that is why there is a this year's model. For anything to get better, it must have had something wrong with it. There is or has been something wrong with everything or we would be stuck in place, driving model-T Fords or sitting around a campfire beating drums. That we have slowly improved almost everything, there must have been something wrong with almost everything.

This book is actually not about what I think is wrong with things. It is about how all individuals have different perceptions of what is wrong, or right, with things. It is also my perception of why things are wrong and the perceptions of people who create or perpetuate the wrong things, rather than change them for the better.

WHO'S RIGHT?

WHO'S WRONG?

ALL PERCEPTIONS ARE DIFFERENT.
WHY IS THIS?

At my present age of 71, I sit at my computer looking at the blank page thinking about how I am going to write this book. The contents are so varied in nature and comprehensive and probably controversial that the task seems daunting.

For many years I have wondered how and why it is that people I know and a great deal of the general public have a different perception of a wide range of topics than I do, or for that matter different from each other. These people have seen what I have seen, read what I have read, observed what I have observed and have varied perceptions. No two people have led identical lives, therefore they have been influenced by different observations, but in general most people are familiar with the same data and still have different perceptions of the same data. Why is this? I assume this is why there are twelve jurors and not just one, but in reality you would think that just one would be sufficient.

It may be perceived that a person who writes a book about himself is self-centered. Actually this book is not about me, but is about the reader and how his perceptions agree or disagree with mine. I am just feeding him baseline information to compare to. If he agrees with me fine, if not, analyze my perception and give it some thought as to why. As I have no agenda or philosophy to adhere to, I am just trying to rationalize things and my rational may be totally incorrect. If it is perceived as incorrect by the reader, he will at least know that there are others out there with the same perceptions as mine, and ask himself, like I have, "How can that be?"

The topics of this book are not so much informative as they are questions and problems that bother me. This is the information I have in my head that I am walking around with and I have formed these perceptions from this information. As these thoughts and remembrances are with me and I do not go to the encyclopedia constantly to verify them to alter my perceptions, and few do, I am not going to the encyclopedia to write this book. I am writing of what I remember and my perceptions at this moment, whether they are right or wrong, with the information I have presently stored in my memory.

I think what troubles me the most is that I have the belief that only a few of the rest of the population out there are troubled or even concerned about such matters. It appears that somewhere there are many individuals who are concerned about select subject matters, but few if any troubled by as many.

Everything that humans have seen, heard, been taught, read about or believe, deserves some scrutiny. I live in a world of, why, what causes that, is that really true, do I understand that, how can that many people be wrong and why? Many of this world's societies, groups of people and individuals are living their lives based on misconceptions and misperceptions, which undoubtedly includes myself. Most of what individuals **think** they know (beyond the absolute irrefutable facts such as 2 plus 2 equals 4 and other absolutes,) are what they **believe** to be true.

As far back as I can remember, I looked at things and questioned why they were like they were. To this day I do the same thing. The amazing thing is that there is someone out there that has the correct answer, but he is living among billions who don't, but believe they do.

All anyone knows is what they observe or are taught. I, like everyone else on the Earth, accumulated this data throughout our lifetime and stored it in our brain as proven data or how we perceive things to be. Proven data is necessary for Engineers, but their perception of what looks good is questionable, although they are pretty certain their perception of what looks good is based upon proven data.

All of what a person observes or is taught during their lifetime and particularly their early life is now what they believe. Albert Einstein pretty well summed it up when he said; "Common sense is the collection of prejudices acquired by age eighteen."

Due to geographic locations, different societies, life styles, economics, cultures and religions, you can easily find millions of people who have the same beliefs and then you can find millions more who are certain the first group is absolutely wrong. Why is this? How can 100 million people be absolutely wrong when they believe they are absolutely right?

*The bottom line is **perception**.* I will try to explain my perception of many topics and questions I pose to myself and others in the content of this book. As the variety of topics or subjects is extensive, I can only write them as I think of them. Therefore the content subjects or topics will be random. As an example, I would like to start with this light subject.

(1) Related events

This is a rarely discussed topic that I give way too much thought. The concept and fact, is that everything I do at any given second will result in different circumstances for the rest of humanity. I call these things that happen *spontaneous events*. Backing up, I often wonder what single event would be so insignificant that it would not eventually affect everything on the Earth in the future. Almost any event will, so I have to think really, really, insignificant. A grain of sand in the Sahara which lodges between others and causes another grain of sand to continue on. That is marginal, but could do it. Somewhere between there and a nitrogen atom bumping into an oxygen atom in the atmosphere is where the event will not change the future of the Earth. This all leads me to where we are and I am today. Had it not been for a rock in an animal trail tens of thousands of years ago, I would not be sitting here today on Earth, as well as the other billions of people who accompany me.

You drop your keys, the future is changed. It takes four pulls on the lawn mower instead of three and the world changes. The larger the event, the faster the change. The event of 9/11 is an example. Events on 9/10 would change the entire future, but they were smaller events and the effects of small events take time to affect everyone, whereas large events take only hours to affect everyone. Events are extremely contagious, as one event creates others and anyone or anything affected by these events creates further events. It is truly a chain reaction.

Because any event changes the world in trillions of different possibilities, one has to look at the history of the Earth and every event and wonder if the most heinous of events may have eventually led to the discovery of small pox vaccine. Millions of people perceive themselves as being so unimportant, poor, wretched or alone that no one will remember them or anything they have done. For these people, I can assure them that they will play a very important part in the future, while there are millions of other more fortunate people pointlessly trying to make a mark for themselves by changing the future. One is a good as the other. This whole scenario creates some obvious psychological problems for people. When grievous things happen, people say "If I had only *something*, this would not have happened." This is absolutely true, but it may have happened sooner or have been much worse if you had done that, *something*. So, everyone is aware of this situation, but they should give it little thought, and that is just as well, or there would be constant traffic jams by people unable to decide whether to turn left or right. This concept could manifest itself as quite a phobia and I am almost there.

You and I have to thank the previous events nearing a googolplex in order for us to be sitting here today. We are here as individuals due to an inconceivable number of events by shear accident or luck. I am not here because it was preordained or it was destiny, but due to a camel relieving himself on a date palm. I could have had millions of different grandchildren, but I have the two I have and they owe their existence to that same camel.

The old phrase, "Well don't blame me." has new meaning when talking about future events. Your mere existence could well have caused the problem. It appears that most people perceive that their existence was determined only by their parents, and I contend they have not given this matter the thought it deserves.

(2) Limited interests

Another thing that I ponder is why people's interests are so narrow. Most people have no interest in anything outside their narrow area of interests. There are millions of subjects, objects, activities and beliefs known to humans. For a variety of reasons, people seem to limit their interest to only a small portion of these. These few interests are compelling and in effect dominate their life. Examples of these would be such as; sports, music, financial gain, cars, religions, drinking, any addictive substance or behavior and etc. This is primarily the reason that U.S. school systems have required varied subject matter. If there were only elective classes, students would intentionally severely restrict their knowledge.

If you decide to write a novel or other literary work, you have to give the matter some serious considerations. Your choice of topic will limit the reading of the novel to a select group of people who have select interests. If your publication is a commercial venture and you have a choice of subject matter, you had better consider the numbers of individuals interested in the subject matter and produce your novel accordingly.

This lack of interest by people in respect to the vast amount of subjects and objects out there has been described as the lack of intellectual curiosity. While a few people have a degree of interest in everything, most people have no interest or curiosity concerning most things. Some people can switch to any channel on TV and watch anything that appears on it, although there are limits to this when trying to watch an episode of "Days of our lives." These people even watch the commercials with some interest. Others switch through 121 channels and say, "There is nothing on."

As what I am writing here, like most other books will be of no interest to people who are already satisfied with their interests in life and do not contemplate there will be many others. This being the case, I may be one of few who will read this book.

For those who have not abandoned this book at this point due to lack of interest, I may be able to coax a few to continue by listing a some of the subjects I am going to discuss, which may fall in their area of interest.

I have questions, comments and perceptions in respect to subjects such as;
Astronomy

Life sciences
Adolph Hitler
Politics
Sports
Societies
American history
Music
Propaganda
Lies
Art
Collectibles
Fishing and hunting
Guns
Global warming
Prejudices
Economics
Health care
Social services
Beliefs
Aliens (illegal and from other worlds)
World history
Sex
Prehistoric times and creatures
National security and the Military
And over one hundred other topics of interest, at least to me.
Although I could write a great deal more about each topic,
perception by nature is a short conclusion concerning
lengthy topics

One would think that of the condensed list of topics
above and one hundred others, there should be something of
interest for everyone. As I stated earlier, this is not a book
attempting to inform people about these subject matters. It is

trying to understand people's perceptions and trying to get an understanding of why people in general do not understand the implications of these subjects due to their own perceptions of them.   Having done a bit of research on a lot of matters in the past, I have conceived opinions and my perception of them, unless I do not understand them at all. These opinions and perceptions are no better than the next persons and can be absolutely incorrect, but I am sure they will be closer than the person who never investigated the matter at all.   There are people out there that have the answers to the individual topics, but their interests are also very narrow and they are scattered all over the world.   Life is too short to research every aspect of these subjects and locating who has the answers. This puts one in the position of arriving at perceptions with what knowledge is readily and easily available. Then you also run into the problem of conflicting information by intellectuals in various groups and cultures.   There is misinformation, when believed by a person or benefits their own self-interest, taints all other available information. For this reason, people have to do the best they can to develop their own perception of any subject and not rely on someone else's perception.

(3) Balance of nature

Now that the perception problems have been discussed, I would like to address the subjects listed earlier as well as others.

I am sure that I am not mistaken when I say that everyone of age has heard the term, The Balance of Nature. As we were taught in school, the informal description or definition of this as taught in the early grades in school; goes something like this. Fundamentally, if you have X amount of foxes and Y amount of rabbits, the balance of nature is when there are just enough rabbits to feed all of the existing foxes. The implication as taught and still perceived, is that in effect the world's wildlife is normally in balance and there are occasional events, which will throw it out of balance. This being enhanced by the Noah's Ark event whereby two or seven of each will work out just fine. My observation and perception of the *Balance of Nature* is that it is a fallacy. There is not now nor has there ever been a balance of nature in the animal kingdom. There are always too many rabbits, too many foxes or too few of one or the other. Not only is it not a viable possibility, in practice it does not work. The end result of this impossibility is usually extinction of a species or near extinction, as has happened for thousands of years. Yes, in many species like foxes and rabbits, the pendulum swings and one always outnumbers the other. And like a broken twenty four-hour clock, it is right once a day and they call that fleeting moment *The Balance of Nature*. What should be taught in schools is *the imbalance of nature, as a normal state of things*. The repercussion of the Balance of Nature perception is that there are environmental laws and beliefs based on the concept that if we leave everything alone it will adjust itself to this balance.

An exception to the imbalance of nature philosophy appears to be in the case of some land animals, where there are extremely vast numbers of a specie. An example would be the case of a vast herd of American bison and their predators the wolves. At one time there were approximately sixty million bison in America. Their natural predators were wolves and some Grizzly bears. Although there were millions of bison, there were never millions of wolves or grizzly bears. We have been taught that the smaller numbers of predators in times of easy pickings will reproduce in accordance with the food supply. This obviously did not happen in the case of wolves although there were a lot of them. Having not heard otherwise, I believe that this is because wolves and grizzly bears are highly territorial. This being the case, there would be a violent conflict between wolf packs and grizzly vs. grizzly if their numbers got too high. This had the same effect as limiting their food supply and therefore limited their reproduction. This is the only explanation for the population of bison to reach sixty million. I guess this could be considered a balance or imbalance of nature, but is not taught in this context.

(4) Sports

Throughout the years, I have watched with interest and curiosity, the numbers of people who are infatuated by games in which a ball of some type is utilized. I have concluded that a ball is used in most sports because it will bounce, roll, and can easily be grasped and thrown, although there were the old head in a sack games, but then again, I guess they would roll to some degree. At any rate, a ball is mobile and not a stationary object. This may be the answer because I can't imagine many games played with a stationary object, but I am sure there are some. I have been known to do some things I enjoy to the extreme, but nothing like games played with these balls. During different periods of the year, the general male population is obsessed with these games to the point that most daily conversation revolves around the games. The fans wear hats, coats and tee shirts bearing the logo of their favorite team. They know which players have a sprained thumb, how far they have run, points they have scored, etc, etc. They call these Stats. I have often wondered why anyone really cares who wins these games, as it will certainly have no effect on any important issues confronting the world or will enhance the life of the fan. Beyond the rational of what difference does it make who wins if they have a good time playing the game; I am totally bewildered by the selection of their favorite team. Asking a hard core fanatical Pittsburgh Steelers fan, "Have you ever been to Pennsylvania?" The reply is "No." I then ask, "Why in the world are you rooting for the Steelers, you have never even been to Pennsylvania?" After a short blank stare, the reply is usually a variation of "I don't know I just like them." There are fans glued to the TV set and yelling and shouting for their team who is in last place and has no hope of being in the super bowl. It seems that most fans have selected a favorite professional team, which they are totally dedicated to. There does not seem to be any rational reason for most of the fans selecting a favorite team and I am extremely curious as to how they arrived at their selection.

The same fans almost exclusively have a logical, rational reason for selecting the college team they want to win and I fail to understand the inconsistency. I must admit that I watch a professional baseball team that I like to see win games, but it is in the state where I live. Makes sense to me, but it really doesn't matter as long as the players are happy playing the game and have enough time off to spend the ten million dollars a year they make chasing the ball.

(5) Pets

You can't go through life without having a certain amount of pets, or if you are rural, domestic animals. The various perceptions people have of different animals are amazing. In the case of dogs, you have the working dogs that are pets and then there are just plain pet dogs. The perception of pet dogs is that they are *mans best friend,* and in the animal world that is certainly true if you are the dogs best friend. One minute your dog can be bringing you your slippers and five minutes later he can be chewing a leg off the mailman. Generally the vast majority of people like dogs. Cats on the other hand are something else, but I have never heard of a cat chewing the leg off a mailman. You have cat haters and cat lovers. Cat haters have no rational explanation for hating them, but almost invariably it is "I don't know, because they are sneaky I guess." I believe that it is instinctive to be afraid of cats because before we had little tabbies, all of the cats were eating us. Being one of the cat lovers, I have to admit that I guess they are sneaky. The perception of being sneaky is easily explained by the fact that cats by nature sneak up on their prey. The other reason is that cats look at humans and recognize the fact that humans are much larger than they are and therefore constitute a threat as they sneak away. Of course domesticated cats and dogs come in all shapes and sizes as well as dispositions. I believe that people are inherently afraid of cats and all unfamiliar large dogs. Consideration must be given to the fact that a high percentage of dogs when confronted by a stranger, will become violent and confront them. Whereas domestic cats will invariably run and hide.

Another interesting thing about pet dog owners is that when they select a pet dog, they select a breed that they can identify with either by appearance or disposition. I guess it is the same as selecting a new car. It's pretty, luxurious, rugged, or 600 horsepower.

Of course there are other pets beside cats and dogs. You have the horse lovers. I am basically an animal person and have read many animal identification books and watched a jillion animal TV programs. The average person has a perception of horses created by what they have seen in movies and TV. Farmers and ranchers have a different view of reality as they deal with horses in their life style. I have a perception of horses, not being a farmer or rancher, which is out of the norm. I perceive horses as being one of the most dangerous of domestic animals. This perception is due to observation and incidents described to me by people who were in close contact with them. Basically it is a battle of wills and the horse is much larger than a human and as smart as some. Thousands of years of being a prey animal has instilled in them a certain degree of instinct in respect to self-preservation. I have heard too many stories about horses purposely inflicting damage to humans to even try to write them. In retrospect it may just be they are getting even with us for thousands of years of mistreatment. I have heard almost as many stories about what was done to horses to make them manageable. Horses as a rule perform tasks because they have to, not because they want to. They want to be on the open range or just left alone. Thousands of years as prey animals has instilled in them a degree of alertness and being spooky to the point that they cannot control their instinctive behavior. Horse people are all too aware of the breeding habits of horses and their inherent violent nature during these encounters. Horses' fighting is not in any way enjoyable to watch and by nature; the males will all fight when in the vicinity of brood mares. They just seem to lose it.

Then you have the pet monkeys, snakes, tarantulas, parrots, lions, cougars, goldfish, wolves, pit bulls, and so on, and the horror stories which accompany these pets. What were these people thinking?

(6) Preferential ignorance

One of the most troubling issues throughout the world population is that they refuse to read, watch or research material which is contradictory to their beliefs or perceptions. This practice at its best is just incompetent behavior and at its worst can create hardships, death and destruction to this planet's population. This practice for the most part has been extreme in human history, as well as today. While this is the case, it can only be contributed to the psychology of the human mind. It is distasteful to read what must be lies, criticism of your beliefs and way down deep there is the fear that researching such information may stain your pure thoughts or somehow hypnotize you into believing some of these lies. More so, it may appear to be unpatriotic, immoral, blasphemy or have other devastating consequences. People do not partake in researching material in contradiction to their beliefs or perceptions, of course, unless they are gleaning material, usually out of context, to fortify their beliefs and to denigrate the opposing position.

The sad thing is that there is a psychological condition whereby the human mind will not accept information contradictory to ones beliefs, regardless of the proven and factual content of the information. The mind refuses to accept a proven fact and it is out of the control of the person with this condition. This appears not to be a rare infliction, but is more common than not in the general population. I will leave it to the reader to research this psychological condition and its name, as it was difficult to locate. My reason for eventually locating it is obvious, as I was curious why people will not believe proven facts, but will easily believe a lie.

(7) Football injuries

This is one of those topics that has a lot to be said about it. Fundamentally the question is, should athletes play football when serious brain injuries are quite common?
The knee jerk response is *No*.
Questions pertaining to brain damage potential by people who play football are; Is the sport in its present form too dangerous to be played at all? Should children be allowed to play football in the school system or for that matter outside the school system? Should the general public encourage the sport by financially supporting it? Who is responsible for these brain injuries and should be liable for these injuries?

I think I will just sit this one out as far as school children playing tackle football as far as an opinion goes. The reality of the situation is that there is a percentage of school football players that are affected by school football brain injuries. I don't have a clue what that percentage is, but it is less than 100% and more than 0%. Whatever this percentage is and it is probably known, it is the responsibility of the parents and the school to determine what an acceptable percentage is. Some parents will absolutely not allow their kids to play tackle football and other parents can't wait for them to play it.

As for professional football, the risk benefit factor is enormously different than for school kids. The risk is significantly greater and the benefits are also. For most professional athletes playing football, they have to make a conscious decision to take the significant risk to make vast amounts of money or not play football and accept what society has to offer them for their other attributes. In almost all cases this will not be being multi-millionaires. In a lot of cases this would actually result in them being in prison because a lot of these players have a hard time staying out of trouble even with their millions, or they just squander the money.

As far as the general public goes, there have been gladiators since the beginning of time and the audience is where the millions come from. I don't think as a rule they really give the problem much thought or care that much unless it is one of their favorite players. They expect a certain amount of pain for their money. Akin to corner seating at the race track.

(8) Hunting in America

This is an interesting topic for me because of my history of hunting and the common mentality of hunters. Being associated with hunters for years and the type people that hunt, there is no doubt that they have a Conservative ideology when it comes to hunting and guns. They have NRA stickers everywhere and badmouth Liberals and environmentalists constantly as wanting to take their rights away from them. Blowing all the ideological smoke away from this subject, I have some thoughts to interject. I will have to say at this point that there are hunters and there are gun ideologues. There are gun ideologues that started out as hunters and there are ideologues that started out as ideologues.

Addressing the hunters and their distaste for Liberals I will say this. If you take a poll of 300,000,000 Americans and ask them if they agree that hunting animals is a virtuous and moral thing to do and should even be done at all, what percentage do you think will say it is not? I will throw a number at you and guess at 90%. Now how often do you hear these 270,000,000 people raising hell about hunters and hunting. There is probably a handful if that. Now why is that? They are supposedly trying to stop hunting and take your guns away and never say anything about it. Now if the 270,000,000 were raising hell, but Congress wouldn't pass such a law, that would be another thing, but that is not it, the 270,000,000 are saying nothing. That is not like 270,000,000 people that disagree with what someone is doing.

Well, I will let the hunters think on this and they can discard these people as being afraid of hunters or the NRA, it has nothing to do with it.

(9) Music

Music is a fascinating thing. I perceive it to be sounds of some duration which have timing and order. I also believe that it is a marker of intelligence and social behavior. I fully understand that there are some birds that have very intricate sound patterns that they duplicate or for some reason change from time to time. The common canary is a master of vocalization which meets all the criteria for music comparable to the best musical instrument. This ability is purely a genetic phenomenon and the canary performs this function with little thought. It is instinctive behavior, which I would like to address later in this book.

As for humans and music, I get the image of early man sitting around a fire beating on a drum in perfect time. His brain is timing each drumbeat to the 1000th of a second. That drumbeat is the human brain analytically doing what it must do. It must have order, and it has the ability. The human body is just following orders and hitting the drum when it has to in order to satisfy the brain. If you don't hit the drum at the given time, it is an indicator that your body or your brain has a problem. The problem may not be severe and is unnoticeable in your society, but down the road somewhere it will have an effect upon you. There is a good example of the brain's ability to subconsciously control humans in respect to sounds. If someone sings *"Shave and a haircut" and* sings no more, your brain will finish the song in perfect timing with no conscious thought from you, *"Six bits."*

Back to the primitive man at the fire beating on a drum. At the same time all over the world, there were and still are primitive men beating on drums. Their brains are demanding it and it is almost hypnotizing, and it could well be hypnotizing. At any rate, the brain loves this rhythm. Are they beating drums or hitting sticks together in rhythm because that is all they have is drums and sticks, I believe so. Probably the fastest technological change in music experienced by humans was due to the enslavement of Africans. These people went from beating drums for thousands of years to playing multi-string banjos in a very short time. That additional several thousand years of beating in time on the drums may have not been wasted, as there is a perception as to the great ability of African Americans in respect to rhythm and this may also have a great deal to do for what is known as Rap.

I am forced to believe that producing quality music on any instrument has a great deal more to do with an individual's brain than a lot of practice on the instrument. I believe that musical ability is inherent in an individual when they are born. You are born with the ability to eventually play excellent music or put it to paper. If you are not born with it, you may be a musician and a good one, but never a great one. History has shown that there have been individuals of extraordinary musical abilities and these abilities were noted at an early age. Symphonies for dozens of different musical instruments have been written by children. I highly suspect that they would have had little trouble entering a profession that required great intelligence, but they chose music, or I tend to think their brain selected it for them. The brain just loves music and the more complex or rhythmic the better.

I spend little time listening to concerts and symphonies and had no real drive to play a musical instrument, which is probably a good indicator as to where I am in respect to inherent talent. Even though we untalented individuals do not generate any music, we love to listen to it. What is remarkable to me is the selection of music people are compelled to listen to. Out of necessity, I accept the possibility that due to my age, I do not have the ability to hear the sounds which make some of these songs very popular. In the case of vocal songs, if the lyrics are sang louder than the accompanying music, I have a tendency to enjoy it more. When the instrumental aspects of a song are considerably louder than the vocalization, I do not have the ability to understand the lyrics. I have many acquaintances who are obviously also endowed with the same hearing impairment as they cannot understand the lyrics either, and the song sells by the millions. The ironic aspect of this situation is that most of the songs I am referring to are playing at about a million decibels and I was always told that these songs would destroy people's hearing. Logic dictates that it has done just the opposite; it has made their hearing better as these people are in the majority and must understand the lyrics perfectly.

I have even caught myself occasionally watching a large symphony orchestra play and as the melody usually does not match my brain's taste for rhythm; I am impressed by the complexity of the whole situation. I can envision a computer writing the music for twenty different instruments playing different melodies or portions at different times and tying it altogether, but not a mere human being. Like a lot of other things, it is not uncommon to determine by the appearance of a person and his wearing apparel, his taste in music.

(10) Lost art

To waver from the previous topic, but not to far, I am distressed by all of the music and motion picture films that are destined for obscurity. A lot of people like myself are guilty of spending countless hours of our life listening to music and watching motion pictures from the early or middle twentieth century. Of course our perception is that those were the good old days and those were the good old films and songs. It would be hard to convince us otherwise. Not to say they don't presently make a few good films and play some good music today, but for the most part the entertainment was considerably different back then and if they make one more vampire movie, I am going to look for a tall bridge to jump from. As a child going to the movies, I was entertained by Johnny Mack Brown, Gene Autry, The Bowery Boys, Abbot and Costello, Lash Larou, and many Looney Toons and Disney cartoons and so on. Those were the movies when a six shooter would shoot about twenty-five times and a horse ran thirty miles wide open. There was a minimum of violence except for fistfights and an occasional cowboy shot from a horse and could be seen to fall for a fraction of a second. For quality entertainment for adults, there were many large production musicals and thousands of well-written, well-orchestrated songs in these movies.

The point I am trying to make about this era and this entertainment is that the young people of today have no interest or curiosity about the entertainment during this era. There were a lot of movies made and music written before my time and although it was not available, I was aware of, Buster Keaton, Al Jolson, other actors and earlier songs. The advent of television made it possible to enjoy or not enjoy them, but they were not lost to me and I watched them out of curiosity. You ask a young person today about these individuals, movies and songs from the past and they have never heard of them, and it appears that they don't care to. It is incomprehensible that it is all lost to the twenty-first century and is just archived to never reappear. Thank God for *Youtube, where we old timers can watch the oldies but goodies and laugh to our hearts content.*

(11) Current entertainment

It is apparent that entertainment has evolved into explicit violence, visual sex content, horror, drug culture, crooked cops and every explicit swear word ever created.

When watching one of these motion pictures, you definitely don't walk away with that warm fuzzy feeling like you used to. It is inconceivable that this does not have a psychological effect upon the individuals watching most of today's films. Their perception of the world has to be significantly different than previous generations. This is to say nothing of the deafening blaring music and explosions.

The alarming thing is that this perceived world on the screen may actually be the world we are now living in, or soon to be living in.

(12) Extraterrestrial life

Enough of the entertainment situation. Let's investigate, *the visitation of an extraterrestrial alien life form,* dilemma. This is a real paradox, due to the fact that the people who should be the most prone to believe in visiting extraterrestrials, are the ones who tend to believe in their existence the least. These people being of religious persuasion.

People of religious persuasion at least believe that there are entities which have visited, or do not live on the Earth surface. Appearances of these entities at times have occurred on Earth and supernatural forces were at work. One would rationally believe that this segment of the population could accept the possibility of some entity not from the Earth's surface appearing on it. This appears not to be the case, as they believe that only the entities that they believe in have done this. Their beliefs make visiting aliens impossibility based upon their belief alone.

Atheists and the like are more inclined to believe in extraterrestrial entities although they do not have the religious individual's perceived proof that this has happened before. Most Atheists believe in the possibility of extraterrestrial visitors, depending on their intellect or knowledge of physics and astronomy. The average red neck Atheist has little doubt as to extraterrestrials and it seems most of them have actually been abducted by them, or may have been abducted. Atheists with little knowledge of physics and astronomy perceive that it would be very easy for aliens to visit us from other planets. Those with greater knowledge of physics and astronomy believe that the anticipated billions of planets in our universe make it almost impossible that there are not other beings on some of these planets. That is the good news, or probably the bad news, and the other good or bad news is the potential possibility of any of them being able to travel to our planet. The most fundamental factor concerning any such possibility is the speed of light, which determines the time element of any astronomical hardware or objects getting from one point to another in our universe. In respect to alien beings, the smart money is on their never having been an alien on this planet. We can be confident that there are no extraterrestrials in our planetary system, which leads the search to our closest stars and their planetary systems to be the best possibility. The SETI project which utilizes sophisticated electronic listening devices such as radio telescopes, has for years been listening for any radio wave transmissions which would be transmitted by an advanced life form. The closest stars being the obvious and then looking further into the Universe. To date, SETI has not detected an intelligence-produced radio wave from outer space. This fact, as well as the time required for any object to travel between solar systems makes it not absolutely impossible for an alien to reach Earth, but would make it absolutely impractical to attempt it.

We are talking about many lightyears of travel for aliens to reach Earth. Of course we have to consider the Warp Drive used by the Starship Enterprise in the television series and the Star Trek movies. Without Warp drive, Star Trek could have never been written. Human beings with life span of a hundred years in an environment that requires thousands of years of travel is not a workable scenario. I am not considering in my thoughts as to the possibility of alien travel, such subjects as time warp, parallel universe, curved universe, black holes, worm holes and so on as they appear to be a little over the edge of safely being of any advantage to a space traveler.

All of this being said, what is my and others perception of UFOs? An amazing number of people believe that UFOs exist. Primarily the reason for this is due to the vast numbers which have been reported, and a great many of these sightings by individuals of high integrity. How can this be explained, if in fact there are no UFOs? Of course a UFO is any object in the atmosphere which cannot be identified as originating on Earth. I cannot confirm or deny what others have seen and would not argue the fact that they had seen it. Myself and millions of others have looked into the night sky for millions of hours and we have never seen a UFO. One scenario is as hard to explain as the other. Knowing what I do of the nature of human beings and the human brain functions, as well as what I know of physics and astronomy; I will put my money with the smart money and say, "No UFOs and no aliens." I do believe that there have to be extraterrestrial beings, but they have just never physically been to Earth.

(13) Instinct

I would now like to address a topic that is one of the greatest mysteries to me. The topic is "instinct." My personal perception of instinct, without looking at Wikipedia is; that it is either inherent data or knowledge within a living organism at the time of conception, or data or knowledge chemically or neurologically acquired during the gestation period. It is easy for a person to understand the physical features of a living organism in respect to genetics and DNA. On the other hand, instinctive traits and actions are for the most part unexplainable. As there have been millions of species of living organisms, there are therefore billions of instinctual behaviors and I have never heard of an explanation of just how this works or is even possible. Learned behavior is understandable, but instinctual behavior is not. As there are these billions of examples of instinctual behavior by other creatures, humans accept it as normal behavior for that creature and give it little more though than that. There have been thousands of studies costing billions of dollars in respect to other creatures and for the most part these studies were to determine the instinctual behavior of other creatures. The end result being an explanation of the effect, but not the cause. The best way to explain the fascinating topic of instinct is to examine some of the effects of instinct on the behavior of creatures. I will attempt to give a few examples that come to mind.

The Monarch butterfly

In February and March in Mexico and southern California, the butterflies mate and then fly north for a few weeks and lay eggs and then die. These eggs hatch (the first generation), they grow and turn into butterflies and continue north. Weeks later, they lay eggs and die. These eggs (the second generation) do the same thing. Weeks later this repeats and (the third generation) continues the journey for weeks, lays eggs and dies. These eggs hatch into (the fourth generation) of butterflies and live for months and complete their journey, which ends back in Mexico and California.

What is amazing about this process is that the original Monarch butterfly starts a migration which will involve four generations in one year and may start in Mexico and continue into Canada and back to Mexico to the same canyon their great grandfather or great grandmother started from. This is as long a journey as thirty-five hundred miles and for the most part they are solitary flyers and not in flocks, so it is apparent that each individual Monarch butterfly has the instinct to accomplish their task.

Another interesting example I am aware of is certain species of pelicans. They mate and lay their eggs on a remote ocean island where the young pelicans hatch out and are fed by their parents. When the young are as large as the parents, but still cannot fly, all of the adult parent birds leave them in isolation on the island that is hundreds of miles from the mainland. All of these parent pelicans go to the same location on the mainland. Weeks later, as the young pelicans acquire the ability to fly, each young pelican makes the long flight to the location where its parents are waiting.

Cases of instinct such as the above are countless in the animal world.

It is pretty obvious that butterflies and pelicans do not discuss flight plans and carry maps, so there is in their brain stored knowledge and brain function which direct their actions.

Besides being bewildered by how the creature is directed, my greater curiosity is in how instinct is passed from generation to generation at the time of conception.

Apparently a single cell has the ability to store all of the instinctive traits of that living creature. There must be one or more genes that contain the instinct data, which eventually becomes a brain function.

Hereditary instinct, which is absolutely not a learned behavior, is perceived by me to be absurd if not impossible, but true. It is not conceivable to me that a young pelican that has never seen anything but a small island can fly hundreds of miles over unknown terrain and water, directly to its parents.

Right or wrong, my perception of instinctive traits is that they are more profound in smaller and more primitive brains. In the case of the Monarch butterfly, that is just about all it has to work with intellectually is instinct. As brain size and functionality increases in living things, they are much more dependent on learned behavior. The human specie having the greatest intellectual capacity, to my knowledge has the least instinctive traits. What may be characterized as instinctive traits in humans seem to be primarily those of self-defense and self-preservation reactions. If you were in a coma at time of birth and awoke years alter in the middle of a highway, everything you looked at would frighten you and you would surely jump out of the way of a car speeding at you. Therefore I believe we have inherent instincts, but they are not as pronounced as in the lower creatures and what we do have, for the most part are replaced by learned behavior. Primitive creatures have abilities a human will never have.

(14) The Summer Solstice

Every June Twenty-first the sun rises and sets just like any other day. The difference being that on June twenty-first the Sun takes longer to travel from horizon to horizon. Hence we have the longest day of the year and it is called the Summer Solstice.   My interest in this matter is one of experience. As the Sun is in the sky longer on that day than any other, wouldn't you think on the average that it would be also the warmest day of the year. It seems that on every June twenty-first I am freezing my butt off and a month or so later I am suffocating from the heat. What is wrong with this picture? This isn't a rare occurrence; it happens every year in that August is hotter than June. I will accept any simple astronomical explanation of why this is, because I do not have a clue. As it makes little sense, I am sure I am not going to be able to figure it out on my own.

(15) Beliefs.

Every one of us has beliefs. My perception of beliefs is, any matter which we are confident is a fact whether based on hard evidence or not.   The bad thing about beliefs is that what one believes may not be a fact and may be absolutely incorrect. I am positive that there is no one on Earth who has a belief, which they consider to be incorrect. Beliefs range in importance such as beliefs you would die for, to minor arguments. There are beliefs in God and country, all the way down to the absolute best colored bass plug. When a subject or object is a proven fact or you perceive it to be a fact, you do not use the terminology, *I think*, you use, *I know* or *I believe*. People tend to use this term, *I believe,* when discussing what they perceive to be true and they have no hard evidence to back it up. The King James Version of the Bible is no more hard evidence for Christian beliefs than the Koran is for Muslim beliefs.   Dying for your country due to patriotic beliefs is another issue as many Nazis' did just that.

As for the best color for bass plugs, now that is really controversial.

The worst thing about beliefs is that the human brain is very susceptible to them. Humans can be taught, brainwashed, indoctrinated, misled, furnished misinformation, propaganda and so on until the individual's brain locks on to this information and it is a belief. Once locked on, depending on the character and logic capacity of the individual, these beliefs may be difficult to impossible to change or correct. Regardless of factual evidence, which may prove the incorrectness of a person's belief, their brain will refuse to accept it. The person's brain will refuse to recognize the evidence and will put a spin on it. A great amount of research has been performed in respect to what I will call a brain disorder. Volumes have been written, but we don't need to read these, just look around you. For these people, the best and most useful tool they have to protect their belief is to refuse to look at the evidence which will prove their belief incorrect.

Good examples are people who have had to be abducted against their will from a cult, and of course there was Jim Jones and his purple kool Aid.

The scary thing is that erroneous beliefs by human beings on this planet run at about one hundred percent of the population. You may believe that you don't have any of these erroneous beliefs, but there you go. You can bet that someone you know with a contradictory belief could point them out to you.

Another negative issue in respect to beliefs is that people are always trying to get another person or persons to adopt their belief. As birds of a feather flock together, this is usually pretty easy. For the birds of a different feather it is almost impossible to convert them. Ironically both groups of birds (in our case being people) are probably incorrect in their beliefs. It is hard enough to eliminate an erroneous belief, let alone reverse one.

You have heard the terminology, die hard Union, die hard Democrat, die hard Republican. Although these statements are made in either a complimentary or uncomplimentary manner, the terminology itself implies that the persons resolve in their belief in that particular group is such that it could never be changed regardless of any issues confronted by the individual. Their brain is locked in.

Another issue I have with beliefs is that I have a lot of beliefs myself, but it just takes hard evidence to change them and I have an interest in looking for hard evidence to do just that. Until there is hard evidence one way or the other, I just accept my beliefs as they are.

Do you believe in UFO,s or Bigfoot? If you say "Yes" or "No", then you just have a belief.

To conclude my perception of beliefs. I **believe** that beliefs are the biggest threat to humanity. Millions have died defending them and millions have died confronting them.

(16) Opinions

Opinions are different than beliefs. An opinion is a belief that has yet to be locked into the brain or the brain refuses to lock it in. It is up for grabs by the brain and has not psychologically been forced into the lock position. Discussing opinions you hear the term *I think*. Opinions are usually based on insufficient information to make a sound judgment and you could be proven wrong. There are people who have a lot of beliefs and few opinions. Having just an opinion is a sign of weakness in their eyes. These are usually the *know it all* people. People of high authority or responsibility, seldom or never use the terminology, *it's my opinion*. These people are expected to know, not have an opinion. These people, who may only actually have an opinion, surround themselves with people who know. This is not always such a good idea because these people bring a lot of baggage with them known as beliefs. People with opinions tend to accept other people's beliefs, because these people seem so sure of themselves.

It is relatively easy to anticipate the actions of people who have known beliefs, whereas it is difficult to anticipate the actions of people with opinions. The reason being is that opinions change frequently and the time of change is difficult to predict. When the individual with an opinion acquires any new information on a subject, the opinion is susceptible to change.

When a vast numbers of people have an identical belief and you are confronted by them socially or militarily, the belief is the motivating factor and we know what it is, and what to anticipate in the way of actions taken on these beliefs. Groups, which are motivated by opinions, are groups which are much less organized and much less fanatical. They are opportunists and function on changing conditions.

(17) Racism and prejudice.

My perception of racism or prejudice of another race, culture or lifestyle is that the explanations are really quite simple and that is why it is such a common trait of people. As racism or prejudice is a learned behavior, it varies to a degree of intensity in each individual.

A simple explanation is when there is another race, culture or lifestyle that an individual perceives to be not up to his standards, beliefs or actions. People have a tendency to believe that every individual in these groups are nearly identical in nature. There would be justifiable prejudices if this were the case. I have no problem with some racism or prejudices if they are in respect to specific individuals or a select group. African -Americans being racists in respect to white Americans is justifiable if this racism is limited to white Americans in the past, and present Americans who have limited their rights to life, liberty and the pursuit of happiness and have oppressed them. As to whites being prejudice against black African-Americans, the same applies. My perception of racism is that in many cases it is justifiable if specific individuals of that race or culture are identified and the standards you expect of that race or culture is justifiable. I would dare to say that the Jews in the world today have good reason to be prejudice or racist in respect to all of the German population who were involved in the Holocaust and the social mistreatment of Jews in Germany and Europe, and those who retain their hatred of Jews. But, the Jews of the world know that there were some Germans, who at great risk to themselves, saved countless Jews from being put to death.

There are great numbers of people who carry with them racial prejudice. This prejudice is developed as a learned trait with dealings or bad experiences with a few and manifests itself until it includes everyone of that race or culture. It tends to progress to a state of hatred. These people are easy to identify by their persistent and hateful comments towards a group. When pressed to be specific and asked if they are referring to every individual in that group, you will get the "Well most of them."

The most pathetic example of racism is the individual who is racist for his own personal ego. Everyone has to be better than someone. People with low self-esteem or for some reason are ashamed of their heritage or position in society, tend to focus on another group which they perceive to be of character below their own. This may not be the case, but it appears that the brain demands it to relieve the stress. After finding others of the same persuasion, or indoctrinating others until they are of the same persuasion, these people inevitably form into groups. I am sure everyone is aware of groups whose basic philosophy is based on racism or prejudice. As a group, these people have found a home and succumb to a state of euphoria as now they feel power and have others in absolute agreement with them. This situation, as compared to being a nobody, is euphoric to the point that they feel that now they are not only better than the other race or group, but now better than everyone who disagrees with them. Hatred breeds hatred and hatred often emulates itself in the form of violent behavior. As racism and prejudice will always exist by the masses, is it too much to ask these masses to at least analyze their own character to understand why they are racists and if there are ulterior motives behind their behavior? Did they acquire sufficient information during their own life to form such a belief or were they indoctrinated to these beliefs?

(18) The Universe.

When I think of the Universe, the first image that pops into my head is that of a Jerusalem sheepherder sitting on a rock looking up into the dark of night. I also imagine prehistoric people, Mayans, Incas, American Indians and all other early peoples doing the same. What were they to think? All they know is what they can see and what they have been told. What they could see is a covering or shell of small bright lights. I am sure a lot if not all characterized these as fires, as that is all there was at the time that emitted light. As some lights were smaller than others and varied in brightness, I assume there was a feeling of depth to the shell by some and to others they were just various size fires. But, whichever the case, there was no comprehension as to the size or extreme depth of the Universe. Even today when thinking of the stars we tend to picture a shell of stars above us. If the matter is given more though than that, our brain kicks into gear and visualizes the Universe as it really is. The structure of the Universe strains the ability of the human brain to the point of incomprehension. What is beyond our expanding Universe is the point where the brain loses it. I don't believe the brain comprehends infinity. It defies everything the brain has seen and has had to deal with during its existence. Eliminating from discussion the potential nothing, which is beyond our Universe, puts my brain to ease. After laying and looking into a clear night sky and trying to wrap one's mind around what one sees and does not see out there, is it just me or do you notice the relief and lack of anxiety experienced by your brain when your thoughts change to Earthly things?

Early man had much less to comprehend when looking at his shell of stars. Although they did travel around the earth daily, their positions were fixed. Early cultures invariably created a reason for them and usually a story about the stars. These stories to be taught to further generations.

Then there was the Sun and the Moon to contend with. The Sun being large and so bright you could not look at it and appeared much closer than the stars. The Moon was the same scenario, but was not as bright and had visible features. These two large objects in the sky were surely the wonderment of primitive cultures and one can only guess at the stories and beliefs of the primitive people watching them. If I was there at the time and was told that the Sun was some sort of God, I am sure I would be on my hands and knees wailing with everyone else. The possibilities for the existence of these objects were extremely limited. Of course during the time of primitive man, there were cultures or groups worldwide and some were much more socially and technologically advanced than others. The more advanced cultures had religious beliefs that explained all of the mysteries of man and the lights in the sky, and other primitive cultures were indoctrinated to these beliefs. Correct or not, it was satisfying to the human brain and the brain was then in its comfort zone.

Looking into the Universe at night at its stationary shining points of light gives one little clue to its nature. With the advancement of technology we have discovered that the accumulated matter in the Universe is hostile beyond belief. We have hot days and cold days on Earth, but the rest of the Universe is composed of objects that are so severe in nature that it is hard to comprehend. All we know that exists in the Universe would kill a human being instantly. Everything is thousands of degrees Fahrenheit or hundreds of degrees below freezing. We are surrounded by objects of extreme temperatures and radiation and a few objects with lethal atmospheres. Is there any place amongst the trillions of objects in the Universe that a human could step onto and survive? It is not known, but it is possible. Are there objects out there which have living organisms on them? I believe there are, but these organisms live in environments which would be lethal to humans. The sheer numbers of objects and the fact that there are living organisms on Earth lends credibility to the distinct possibility that there are living organisms on other planets or moons. As for the possibility of one of these being habitable by humanoid types, in my opinion there is one or *more*. What does *more* mean, when there are billions or trillions of planets with the potential? Whether resembling human beings or not, intellectual beings are highly possible. Observing the diversity of the planets and moons in our solar system and the discovery of many others outside our planetary system indicates that there are a near infinite variety of planets and moons with different characteristics. If in our small solar system there are planets or moons that can conceivably sustain living organisms, then outside our solar system there are a near infinite number of very good possibilities. Our early life forms evolved to survive the conditions of the Earth and its environment at a time that would have killed a human instantly. Another extraterrestrial body with different characteristics would undoubtedly require quite different life forms than ours.

Setting aside the Creationist belief as to the origin of the Universe and human beings, an interesting thought has to be given some consideration. This thought being, if by chance the Earth had a duplicate in the identical orbit of Earth, so that all of the identical astronomical conditions existed, what would you observe if you were to travel to it today? Would it be as barren as the moon and we are just a freak of the Universe? Is it possible that the Earth and its duplicate, due to their location are destined to have living organisms, which were created by the conditions they were under? It could well be discovered that certain planets and moons have no choice in the matter of obtaining life forms. It will inevitably happen if they are in the rare sweet spot in a solar system. Does it even matter if life has occurred on other planets or moons? *No*, is more likely than *Yes*, due to the distance which is between these planets or moons with life on them. The distance between them makes it a mute point in respect to physical contact. It is possible that we could receive a "Hello", but any reply by us would take hundreds to thousands of years. Our reply would probably arrive at a civilization which no longer existed and probably did not exist when we received the "Hello." The futility of the situation is obvious.

For the fundamental Creationists, the answer to all of this is quite simple; we are discussing something, which is not possible. It is very definitive what the situation is in respect to the existence of man and there is no need to look further. God created everything as it is and humans were created on Earth. If this is the case, we are truly wasting our time and money on any space exploration looking for humans. Genesis does give some religious Liberals a little leigh way as to its interpretation. For years religions have resisted these possibilities and are bending with the wind in respect to astronomy and the existence of living organisms on distant objects in the Universe. The Catholic religion appears to be taking the lead as to astronomical observations and these possibilities. Genesis taken as record of factual events, created a situation where you had to fit science in where you could. It appears that now we are at a point that science is a fact and now we fit Genesis in where we can. As Genesis is a belief, no amount of science will alter its credibility, as any new astronomical discoveries will just be incorporated into it. The Creationists could well be right in respect to the Universe and it was in its entirety created by a supreme being. The Creation began as the Big Bang as a planned event and was a grand scheme of things. Did Earth's story and its inhabitants play out on many planets in the Universe, who knows?

I am an individual with some interest in astronomical studies and endeavors, but I can see the futility of any benefit of investigating the Universe outside out solar system which would lead to intelligent beings having any communication or physical contact with Earth.

(19) Health care for citizens.

From the time of earliest man; health care has been a concern for humans. In the most primitive tribes, whether they are at present or twenty thousand years ago, they practiced or practice various forms of organized health care. In the case of the primitives it was usually the function of a medicine man or a person comparable to this in any culture. There is enough evidence to support this in prehistoric times as well as in historic times.

In my opinion, early health care given to humans was limited to humans which were known to each other. I have not heard of any cases of health care givers, medicine men or whoever, out searching the area of a conflict for injured enemies to heal. The evolution of these early healers to our present day doctors has been a long one. The more socially and intellectually advanced we have become, the more aware we are that the enemy is very similar to ourselves and the more sympathetic we become to his health or injuries. In recent history, treating injuries of ones enemies has become more common. But still, ones interest in becoming involved in caring for or healing other peoples, to a degree is dependent upon how similar they are to us. White Americans become extremely concerned about health problems in Europe, whereas in Somalia it is of less interest or concern.

Throughout history, the rich and the famous have always had the best health care that was available at the time. In this matter, little has changed.

Man has always been at the mercy of human contagious diseases. The Bible speaks of these and the fate of many American Indians of both North and South America was an example of the danger of these diseases. The isolation of human societies from each other until the last several hundred years was the primary defense against these diseases. As the technology of transportation of people advanced, as well did the diseases and the study of medicine and cures for these diseases. This advancement in medicine was fortunate, as today there is no isolation of societies or groups of peoples.

Currently our situation worldwide is that a new virus or plague in any part of the world is confronted as if it were in the house next door.

In the third world countries, people are dying by the millions and the fatality rate diminishes in the richer and more technologically advanced countries. Although millions die every year in the countries of this higher status, they are dying at an older age and of medical conditions which are extremely stubborn or impossible to cure with the technology presently available. As an example, in the United States our medical treatment abilities are such that if you have access to the treatments that are available, you have a good chance of living into the eighties. Of course some drop by the wayside before then and some live much longer. A great deal depends upon whether or not you have the available health care and how well you take care of yourself. This being the case, most modern developed countries have some form of Universal Health Care for its citizens. Some countries sooner than others, and the health care programs vary greatly.

The bottom line though is that societies have concluded that living or dying based upon financial or social position is not a workable scenario. The reasons for it not being a workable scenario are numerous as we have moral and social consequences to consider. Can a society continue to function if there is a large segment of it aware that they or their loved ones may die because they cannot afford the treatment available? I think not. Due to our advanced communication abilities today, there is an awareness of what is treatable in respect to illnesses and the medical treatments that are available. It is accepted by the population that there is a difference between a bottle of generic antibiotics with instructions and a doctor at your bedside administering more effective antibiotics. The privileged can have a doctor at their bedside and that is acceptable, but every citizen should be able to have the bottle of effective antibiotics. Anything less than this will surely create social disorder.

If there is a person or group in America who would deny a father saving the life of his son or daughter, I can foresee a great problem for these people. Universal health care in a society may have less to do with morality than it does with self-preservation of the wealthy.

The major problem in America is that the cost of a universal health care system, or you can call it socialized medicine, is that it is cost prohibitive under our present social structure. Our current medical system exists today due to a variety of factors. A stand-alone hospital system is not possible due the vast numbers of people requiring medical assistance every day. This system would require hospital structures larger than any structures on the planet. Can one imagine every person in a city who has an appointment at one of the hundreds of clinics or medical professional offices, showing up at the same structure or building at any given time? Thousands of patients per hour would be showing up at these immense structures.

As the knowledge of medicine has advanced dramatically, it was obvious that physicians had to specialize in a specific field of medicine. The general practitioners became obsolete as someone who treats all ills, but there are many still practicing today and play a major role as one who can prescribe medicine, and give people referrals to specialists. Our hospitals today function as locations for having major surgery, emergency rooms, a birthing center, people requiring intensive care and people who require overnight treatments. Almost all other medical services are performed in the hundreds of modern, artistic, expensive, well-groomed clinics dispersed throughout the cities. This is in fact a very efficient system and is why some people claim that America has the best medical system in the world, although others would argue this point. This system works beautifully when everyone has health insurance or is on Medicare or some other social program. When it does not work, is when everyone does not. An example of this is when any doctor's office or general practitioner is contacted by someone with a health issue and is not insured. There will probably be no appointment made and no referrals. Usually the person is pointed in the direction of a Minor Emergency building or a hospital Emergency Room. There are financial issues concerning both of these locations. Not having health insurance and prescription drug insurance is a heart wrenching position to be in. Most of us are not familiar with this horrible situation, particularly if an infant son or daughter is involved.

Preventing this horrible scenario, basically by overcharging those with funds and social programs has prevented a devastating situation of social unrest. For a variety of reasons, these social programs are becoming unsustainable. My perception of the problem looming before us is that we have to restructure our medical system as Henry Ford did for the auto industry, or at least have a minimal Universal Health Care system which covers all citizens. This is where the people who give the problem the least amount of thought jump up and say, "Citizens, they aren't even citizens." This is another issue to address later and my thoughts here only refer to U.S. citizens.

There is a large group of people out there who have no concept of repercussions to activity or inactivity. I would suggest to these people that the health care situation be given some thought as to the potential repercussions. Health insurance is not the only kind of insurance in the world. There is insurance to maintain America's society and life style.

This is where my perception of the health care situation differs from some others. If we do not satisfy the situation to at least a minimum which all citizens can tolerate, they *won't* tolerate it. Voting different people and parties into office to many seems to be the fix, but in reality the winners of these elections will eventually be the ones in office when the shit hit's the fan.

It is no surprise to me that the United States is the last major player to adopt a health care system. Most Americans do not want to spend their money to heal someone else; of course unless it is a friend or someone they like. The position that illegal aliens are responsible for our dilemma is only true to a small fraction of the cost. Like most others, it is my opinion that our present health care system is a good system if you do not have to pay for your medical bills out of pocket. Almost everyone also agrees that Medicare is being severely abused by the private sector and as well by many Medicare and Medicaid patients. It is difficult for a Medicare patient to leave a medical facility without a future appointment, whether they need it or not. On one occasion, I had to spend ten hours in a hospital Emergency Room for tests and a diagnosis. The bill was $16,000.00 and Medicare paid the bulk of it. That is $1,600.00 per hour. The abuses to Medicare are too many to list. The charges can be justified in most cases because someone has to pay for all of those new multimillion-dollar clinics and hospitals being built and maintained.

Politically, there is little interest in doing anything but cutting Medicare and Medicaid benefits in lieu of cutting the waste, astronomical drug prices, mismanagement and some fraud.

Any other actions will be stepping on some ones toes and is not good for the private sector. In the extreme, if Medicare and Medicaid were to be eliminated, and there are some who think this to be good fiscal policy, our society in this country would be devastated. What would these consequences be?   An hour pondering the situation and listing the consequences should be done by anyone considering cutting Medicare and Medicaid expenditures to excess.   As these programs are a safety net for the less wealthy, they are also a safety net for the wealthy against the possible repercussions.

(20) National security and the military

I perceive that the number one priority for the U.S. Government is the security of the nation.   Without this security nothing else matters. Peace and pacifism, as well as unnecessary military aggression because we can, are two philosophies of which one is no better than the other. The bottom line is that regardless of the cost, the United States should be in a position to destroy any or all nations who plan to destroy us. As we go, so go our enemies.

If there is an area of excellence in performance by the United States, it has been the defense of this nation and that was not always the case. World War Two was the defining factor in our resolve to defend the U.S. from enemies abroad. Historical military events and battles during World War Two were won and lost and there was a great deal of uncertainty and luck involved.   There was a distinct possibility that Japan could well have invaded Australia as well as the United States.   No one knows what the final results would have been if this had taken place. This possibility was a real eye opener to the American public and was not soon forgotten.   Convoys off the East Coast could be seen bursting into flames due to German U-boats just off our shore. In the early nineteen forties, it became all too clear that if we survived this World War, another one would be unacceptable.   Every American has heard the title, *"The*

Greatest Generation." This being the generation of young men and women who made every sacrifice and braved every danger to themselves to defeat our enemies during World War Two. I am a true believer in the *Greatest Generation,* but I take nothing away from any other generation which has defended the U.S. Putting one's life at jeopardy is the same regardless of the generation. I think they were *The Greatest Generation* because there were so many who were not fighting for a philosophy, but were fighting to prevent the very possible destruction of the U.S. and the lives of their families back home. Of course in the midst of heated battle, this is out of one's mind and self-preservation and the preservation of your buddies fighting at your side is your objective.

Post World War Two and the Iron Curtain standoff with the Soviet Union is an example of what had to be done regardless of the cost or risk. The entire scenario of throwing yourself under your school desk and covering your head, nuclear bomb shelters, disaster shelters, incoming missile sirens, etc, etc, is an experience our younger generations have had the good fortune to miss. It left a distinct impression on my perception of world affairs and consequences of dealing with nuclear-armed adversaries.

Since World War Two, armed chair strategists, politicians, misinformed people and people with an agenda have adopted a perception of the military conflicts since that time. The worst of these individuals is the one who agrees with many others about these conflicts in a cynical manner because it is fashionable or politically correct. This is the case in the conflicts in Korea, Vietnam and the Middle East. Korea being so long ago that most do not remember the conflict, but are aware we did not win a victory and therefore we had no business being there. Vietnam is the ultimate in being critical of a war so as to be politically correct. The general public will almost all agree that it was a mistake to be there so as to be in agreement with everyone else. I have researched the cause and effect of both of these wars and I again wonder about my perception of things. I understand perfectly why we were in Korea and Vietnam. In my mind our involvement was a logical decision in both cases due to the situation at the time.   I don't agree with every aspect of how we fought these wars, but I have no question as to why we were there. Why am I, the government and military at the time, so far out of touch with the majority of today's U.S. citizens on this matter? Why is, or was, our perception of things different from these citizens?   If my perception in respect to these wars is correct, what we have is a country full of people who; are good hind sighters, are politically correct, only like winners, just agree with the masses, or have some type of socially enriching agenda.

If the government and I were wrong at the time, we misjudged the ferocity, brutality and the intent of the Communist philosophy at the time. I tend to believe that there was a misjudgment on my part alright, and this being that the Communist aggressive situation was actually worse than I thought.   As for Afghanistan and Iraq, they differ from Korea and Vietnam in that Korea and Vietnam were bordered by the then antagonistic Chinese super power with very hostile potential worldwide.

Our *first* conflict with Iraq was a logical and necessary response and I have no problem with that conflict or how it was handled. Schwarzkopf, Powell and every person in the military performed a marvelous job. It appears George Bush analyzed the situation well and we exited the conflict in an orderly manner. As for the Highway of Death, you reap what you sow. It is amazing how public opinion is overwhelmingly in support of a winner. There is no whining about that conflict regardless of why we were there.

As for Afghanistan and the second Iraq war, there seems to be two opposing groups out there today. The first group doesn't even want to talk about why we are there and the expense to date, and the second group wants us out of there with a win or at least a little bit of pride.

The first group does not want to talk about how both wars were mismanaged, how they were able to manage the Congress and get the public to participate. The second group has made the story all too clear, but we are still there.

As for myself, I find it hard to pass judgment on the necessity to invade Afghanistan or Iraq. If four people ever needed killing it was Osama Bin Ladin, Saddam Hussein and those two deviant sons of his.

We entered these two countries with a righteous philosophical mindset as to how thing should be and we encountered how things really are.

(21) Homosexuality and bisexuals

The fundamental argument in respect to homosexuals is why we have them at all. Is it a genetic trait or a learned behavior? The religious community subscribes to the theory that it is *learned* deviant, unnatural, ungodly behavior. I suspect this is due to the fact that humans, having originated from God, homosexuality may have some negative reflection on the creation. The Bible makes reference to humans inclined to be homosexual and an interpretation of God's thoughts is that this is a negative thing. I don't think anyone asked God right out, but someone must have known God's thoughts on the matter because it is in the Bible.

My perception of the evidence I have come in contact with is that it is a genetic trait whether created by God or not. Earlier in this book, I questioned whether Adam had mammary glands, as all male humans do today. If I knew this, I may have different perceptions as to homosexuality. If Adam did, it was by God's design and if Adam did not, it is a genetic deviation in today's males, probably caused by the combining of a male cell from Adam and a female cell from Eve. A situation which may or may not have been anticipated as per Genesis.

There is little question that mammary glands are a more prominent and useful trait of female mammals. The purpose for the glands is also not questioned. This being the case, human males must carry a genetic trait of females. Is this the only female trait that males have? My observation of thousands of males and their physical traits, for me is inconclusive. I am quick to pick up the characteristic traits of most homosexuals. They are openly obvious. Is this caused by female traits in a male? I don't know, but I believe so. Female homosexuals tend to have male features. In both cases there are medical processes which can enhance these features dramatically to the point of sex change.

I have no prejudice for or against these homosexuals, as they are no more responsible for how they look or act than I am. There are some disturbing character traits of homosexuals that I am aware of. One being that their sex drive appears to be greatly more intense than normal males, which in itself is hard to believe. Their sexual activity is extremely prolific to the point that hunting and fishing would have to take a back seat to their sexual activity. I would almost call it obsessive behavior. The gay bars, meetings with whoever is at the park at the time, risky unlawful solicitation, molestation of small boys, etc, etc.

The homosexuals normally observed are behaving far beyond what a normal heterosexual couple would be doing on the street.

By the same token, there are many cases of two homosexuals who are cohabitants for years with little attention drawn to them, until they want to get married. Now this is a real problem for almost all of the people who are not homosexuals. The homosexuals who want to get married are not content with some kind of partnership agreement or legal document. These are the ones who irritate the hell out of most people and particularly the religious factions. Regardless of what the public or I may think, it is merely a legal matter, which can or cannot be justified by written law of a State or the Federal Government.

If a law defines marriage as a legal agreement between **two people,** which is titled a Marriage License or agreement, there is no legal reason they cannot get married. As to the constitutionality of preventing such a marriage, not allowing it may be discriminatory.

As to the morality of such a marriage which is questionable due to public perception of their gender, lifestyle and sexual behavior , this seems to fly in the face of religious beliefs.

As most religious people agree that it is a learned trait, there is the fear that other normal children may be influenced by them and become homosexuals. The numbers of homosexuals leaders within the religious community should give these people food for thought as to the learned trait theory. And for that matter the ability to change from homosexual to a straight male, forty years of teachings of the gospels did not change homosexuals in the religious community, back to straight.

Male inmates in prisons who practice sexual acts with other males do not become homosexuals. My perception being that homosexuals are born as homosexuals, lends a little sympathy to the religious homosexual. Homosexuals have no choice in the matter and condemning him is not a moral act either. If a normal heterosexual male was told that he was to live his life with no sexual contact with a female because it is immoral, this would not work either. Talking people out of satisfying instinctive self-preservation acts and sex drive traits is difficult. That is your reason for being here. There is no question that a homosexual can suppress his desires and actions and live the life of a heterosexual and this must be very difficult indeed. In some of these cases it is merely a matter of denial.

Bisexuals are somewhere between heterosexuals and homosexuals. This whole matter has to make us consider that we are all somewhere between being pure heterosexual and pure homosexual.

(22) Conspiracy theories.

Everyone has heard of or listened to conspiracy theories. These theories relate to incidents which cannot or have not been proven to the satisfaction of the general public. In almost every case, the origin and continuation of conspiracy theories can be traced to individuals who profit by such theories. Books are written, movies are made and there are countless television documentaries concerning the matter. Some of the most prominent conspiracy theories are such as; who really assassinated Kennedy, Roswell, Bigfoot, both Roosevelt and G. W. Bush were aware of an impending attack on the U.S. and did nothing to stop it.

There is reason to believe that it is not impossible that one or all of these theories are true. That is why these theories linger around for decades. The information pertaining to the theories is in itself not credible, but they cannot be disproved. I have watched, read and listened to these conspiracy theories and if the people who are promoting these theories really believe them, they would certainly show us the proof that made them true believers. Like everyone else, I have been asked if I believe in specific conspiracy theories. While many people say, "Yes" or "No", the truth is that they do not know. My perception of conspiracy theories is that until they are proven correct, I am going to assume they are not. There may be good reason for the controversy over these incidents, but I have nothing to add to the credibility of them.

(23) Humor

I am always amazed at what various people consider humorous or funny. I can accept the fact that like beauty, it is in the eyes of the beholder. I cannot help but think this may be a reflection of a person's life experiences. I am sure that there have been people whose life experiences have been so tragic that they are not capable of the luxury of humor. One's ability to appreciate and enjoy specific humor is a learned trait and has a great deal to do with a person's surroundings and family and friends during their early life. Being raised in a family where humor was a good part of the communication process, I tend to see the humor in about everything. This may be a personality disorder on my part, but it tends to make life easier for me. I know people with an opposing disorder and they are not a lot of fun to be around.

Different people obviously do not have the same perception of what is funny. A good example and one used a lot is a movie where a person is slipping on a banana peel. Some think this is humorous and others see no humor in it at all. If you do not think it is funny, you do not appreciate the content of the story or personalities of the people it is happening to. In fact, you probably would not find the entire movie very funny. Although I have somewhat of an eye for humor, there is the comic strip called Snoopy that I have read for years and have as yet to crack a smile. I have thought, maybe an eight-year-old would think it was funny and then I think, nope, millions of people love this comic strip. When I continue down the rarely visited comic page, I read more of the strips and they aren't funny either. I think the cartoonists ran out of material about thirty years ago.

As a comparison of my perception of humor, I will list some of the comedians or actors who I think are or were funny. Not all of their work and not all of the time, but generally. Laurel and Hardy, Peter Sellers, W.C. Fields, Wiley Coyotee cartoons, Jack Lemon.

Far from being a prude, I don't appreciate the comedian or comedy material which is usually composed of outrageously profane dialogue. I can see the humor in it, but I want to be in a room by myself with earphones on when I watch it. After a short time I lose my taste for it all together. If you are in the audience listening to it, you have to laugh, what else can you do? I consider having a sense of humor a gift. It is how one gets through life with the least amount of stress. There are enough people out there without this gift (sourpusses) that you will need a sense of humor just to contend with them.

(24) United States national resources (2011)

One of the best-kept secrets or information just not publicized, are the natural resources within the United States. The popular perception is that we get almost all of our oil from other countries and some from Alaska and the Gulf Coast and some natural gas from Canada. The obvious reason must be because we do not have any here. In reality, the amount of oil, gas and coal within our borders is beyond belief. We will have billions of barrels of oil in the ground when the other countries go dry, with the exception of Russia. The reason it will be in the ground is that our system of recovering fossil fuels is to lease the resources to large oil companies who lease the resource area and/or pay us a royalty for what they pump out of the ground and sell worldwide. Most of our vast oil resources will be difficult and costly to recover, but not unprofitable with gasoline at $4.00 per gallon at the pump.   The recovery will require some new technology and up front financial investment. This technology should already have been developed years ago and some of the multibillions we have paid the Arabs for years should have been used to develop the recovery systems.   Why hasn't this happened?   It is really pretty simple. The U.S. has made it possible for the oil companies to jump around and hi-grade the oil deposits.   The easiest and the most profitable has always been their next move. Are we at their mercy?   All indications are that we must be. The obvious thing to do for the U.S. Government, who represents the citizens, is to develop the vast oil deposits within the U.S. ourselves. We would not be the only country in the world that does this. Maybe we could put some of those NASA people back to work. Or would this be too socialistic and we would all go to hell for doing it? If we don't pursue this technology and ability now, we are going to get caught with our pants down when the Arabs shut off the spicket.

The last time the news was out about the massive U.S. oil reserves and pilot plants were being built, which was year's back, the price of Middle East oil plummeted. I suspect the same thing would occur again. Be assured that the large oil companies, corporations and foreign governments are not friends of the U.S. citizens. We have a lot of money and they want it.

I hesitate to mention the methane hydrate deposits off our coasts because it scares the hell out of me, and for good reason. You might Wikipedia, *U.S. Methane Hydrate deposits.* As a note, Methane Hydrate deposits may play more of a factor in your life than as a fuel source.

(25) Pure democracy

The general population of the United States perceives that we are living in a pure democracy. This is not correct, as our form of government is a Democratic/Constitutional Republic, which I will address later. A pure democracy is where every individual has a vote and no one represents the voters. The only known case of a pure democracy in history was on the early pirate ships in the Blackbeard era. The captain had no power over the crew. All decisions were made by the crew and voted on. The captain did have the rank as military leader in the heat of battle, but that was the limit of his authority. This tidbit is just a break from more wearisome topics.

(26) Intrinsic values

This is a topic of interest to me and I assume to others. What is intrinsic value? My perception of it, which may differ somewhat from your dictionary, is as follows. A painter takes a $5.00 piece of stiff fabric, spreads around $2.00 worth of paint on it and the picture is downright awful, and puts a for sale sign on it reading $20.00. The painter next to him does the same thing and his painting is also terrible, but his for sale sign says $2,000,020.00. The first guy was named Smith and the second guy's name was Picasso.

The difference between $20.00 and $2,000,020.00 is the difference in intrinsic value. It is the premium you pay for a particular object and intrinsic values are usually associated with collectibles. One man's treasure is another man's junk and the treasure price is intrinsic value. All of us watch TV programs like The Pawnshop, The Pickers, The Road Show etc. Repeatedly you hear what the pawnbroker anticipates he can get for an object and you persistently hear, "At auction it could go for." Like me, do you wonder who is buying all of this stuff at thousands to tens of thousands of dollars?

(27) Write a book

Well, everyone wants to write a book. There are several reasons people want to write a book and one being that it is something that will outlive them. There are several problems here and the first is that there are people who can and people who can't write a book. One person sits at a word processor and writes a sentence or two and they go blank. Others sit at a word processor and it is like turning on a water spicket, it just keeps flowing. People with a vivid imagination never run out of fiction material whereas those with little imagination have little to write about. Another issue is attention span and those with a short one have trouble embellishing the same subject for any length of time.

My thought on the matter is that everyone should write a book and as well they should be prepared for disappointment and a nightmare.

There are millions of uncompleted books out there and millions of completed books that will never be read. Unless you have a specific group to give them too, you had better be going through the procedure for self-satisfaction.

Warning! If you write one, be prepared for the self-abuse of writing another.

(28) Global warming (2011)

My knowledge of global warming is based upon what I have read, what I have seen and what knowledge I have of chemistry and physics. I have read volumes in respect to the causes and effects of global warming. Most of the evidence I have read for the existence of a global warming effect appears to be quite legitimate. The multitudes of temperature measurements lend credibility to its taking place. The argument for the existence of global warming has been scoffed at and belittled by a large segment of our society. Not because there was not enough definitive proof, if they had taken the time to examine it, but for philosophical and political reasons. This criticism was for the most part due to the theory that it was being caused by fossil fuel emissions. If believed, this was not in the best interest of people involved in industry. Other skepticism was no more than being in philosophical opposition to the people who were making the claims.

This denial has slowly evolved to an unapologetic, "Ok, we are having global warming, but emissions are not contributing to it."

As for myself and what time I have spent below the Arctic Circle, like others, I cannot see any effects of global warming in the Lower Forty Eight/Nine. We are having weird weather, but we have had weird weather before. If it were not for my experiences of seeing the changes in the far north and above the Arctic Circle, I may be open to argument against the severity of the global warming we are experiencing. Only the people in the far northern and far southern latitudes are seeing the drastic effect global warming is having on Earth. The changes which are being experienced in the far north and south will have serious effects upon every continent on the Earth. The severity of these effects can be moderate for the next fifty years or so, or they can be catastrophic. In fifty years the Earth may not be able to sustain the existing human population numbers. That scenario is bleak to say the least, particularly if you are a new father.

What was earlier the argument that this was a normal cycle that the Earth goes through is conceded by most of the scientists and their position is that we are merely adding to this probable normal cycle with our fossil fuel emissions. The greenhouse effect is a phenomenon, which is not a theory. This greenhouse affect has happened many times in the history of the Earth as has the ice ages. My understanding of the nature of ice ages or mini ice ages is that they can evolve in a period of less than twenty years. If global warming repercussions are anything like the quick conversion to an ice age, we could be in big trouble in the short term. Unless there are a lot of liars out there, there is definitely a difference in perception as to the significance of fossil fuel emissions. We have all of the significant data about the Earth's atmosphere for the last several decades. We know the quantities of fossil fuel emissions because we have measured the emissions in the atmosphere. We know that these emissions will unquestionably cause an accumulation of heat on the Earth's surface.

What the scientific community cannot prove, even with the use of computer modeling, is the exact amount of heat accumulation over a period of time. This is primarily due to the normal imprecise cycles of temperature variation on Earth as well as the varying amounts of emissions, whether manmade or natural. That being the case, the temperature rise cannot be precisely determined over a period of time, although there is little question that it is rising. Well, this is good enough for the group who has an interest in doing little or nothing about global warming. They just say that the scientific community cannot prove their theory. I suppose they are correct if you can satisfy yourself that the Earth will be going in to a cooling cycle, which offsets the greenhouse effect of fossil fuel emissions. When is enough evidence, enough? If your brain is locked on to a philosophical disbelief in global warming, there will never be enough. People have died by the millions because they were living in a repeating disaster zone, as their brain refuses to accept the inevitable.

(29) The Gold Standard.

At one time in U.S. history, you could say we were on the Gold Standard. An ounce of gold was around $20.00 and a twenty-dollar gold piece weighed an ounce and a $10.00 gold piece a half ounce and so on. During that time there was and still is a law we have all heard of that makes it illegal to deface money. What they were talking about was not hitting it with a hammer, but were talking about a practice which was taking place where small slivers of gold were cut from the coin which remained a $20.00 gold piece and then selling these slivers by weight. Paper money was gold certificates payable by gold on demand. We also had silver certificates payable in silver on demand. Of course this required fixing the price of gold and silver regardless of the quantities available or the changing cost of mining it. All paper money had to be backed by gold or silver. I have forgotten the particulars, but it does not require a good imagination to understand that eventually more money was required than could be backed by gold. So, you raise the price of gold to $35.00 per ounce, no more, no less.

For a variety of valid reasons we broke away from the Gold Standard. At some point, in the twentieth century, the U.S. Government required that almost all of the gold in the U.S. had to be turned into the government. I wish my memory was better, but I am thinking that is why we have the vast accumulation of gold in Fort Knox. This would be an interesting bit of research for someone out there. I have done it and have forgotten it.

Well anyway, for years there have been groups of people who want to go back on the gold standard whereby our money is backed by gold. Their thought is that this will eliminate the inflation issue and will prevent the Federal Reserve from printing money by the truckload. Usually these are people with great wealth who would like to protect their wealth with a no risk commodity. A commodity which is accepted worldwide as a medium of exchange. This makes sense, but of course the price of gold would increase rapidly as there is just so much gold available. This group already has the gold and just can't wait for the value of gold to increase one hundred fold.

Then of course there is the problem of production. Every ounce recovered out of the ground would be of great value. In short order a small African country and Russia would be the wealthiest countries in the world. What is the point in that?

This is my perception of going back on the gold standard and I know there are many out there that have a perception different than mine. They could be right. I might say to them though, "We *are* on the gold standard, go buy as much of it as you want. It is good anywhere."

(30) Type A and type B personalities.

I have read a great deal in respect to type A and type B personalities and I am walking around with a lot of information in my head about type A and type B personalities. The following is my perception and conclusions in respect to this information, which may or may not be accurate, but it is what I am functioning with.

Are there type A and type B personalities walking around? Certainly there are, I know a lot of both types and have a tendency to judge people as to their personality types. Actually there is a type C personality, but I am leaving them out of this, and trust me, they won't care.

Actually type A and type B personalities are at the end of a spectrum with varying degrees in between. My understanding and perception of a type A individual is as follows. They are by nature more aggressive, competitive, ambitious, talk persistently, easy to infuriate, very social, seek personal wealth, popularity and importance, are pissed off and don't know why and are always right. You know the type. Type A.

These people are the people who go into a rage when another driver does something the type A does not like, even though the type A does the same thing all of the time. You will see the type A frequently in the political arena or carrying signs and yelling at the other type A across the street. Type A people tend to be almost over the edge in any endeavor they pursue, whether it is cars, trucks, religion, sports, social events, alcoholic beverages, rowdiness, and are extremely opinionated. There are more character traits and the type A I am describing is at the extreme end of the spectrum. Type A people are not bad people, in fact they are quite generous, caring, and have numerous friends.

Now type B personalities on the other end of the spectrum, can be described as laid back, order right off the menu, not aggressive, think before they jump, are less violent in nature, look at the driver who does something stupid and thinks, "I have done the same thing" are less competitive, find it difficult to be rude, less opinionated, and for the most part just about everything the type A personality is not.

Of course almost everyone falls into the spectrum between the two extremes. Everyone knows people who show these tell-tale signs of their type A and type B characteristics. Type B personalities are quite uncomfortable around type A personalities. It is like they have to go into double time just to stay up with them. Leaping before you look makes a type B uncomfortable, but that is where he is when with a type A. Type A personalities on the other hand are quite comfortable around the type B. They are a little irritated because the type B just don't seem to get the obvious and they seem to have to lead the reluctant type B around. The reality of the situation is that the prisons are full of type A personalities and the type B people go visit them. It appears to me that how a person gets through his life is dependent upon where he is located on the spectrum. Type A personalities are destined to have more problems because of their personalities than type B personalities.   Most things are a problem for type A personalities anyway, as everything can't go a person's way all of the time. I suspect most divorces can be attributed to a type A and type B marriage. Type A and type B people can be good friends, but it requires a lot of tolerance from both. Type A and type B personalities are a function of the brain, which I am going to address later.

(31) Separation of church and state

If Americans have learned nothing else in the last 300 years, they should have learned the necessity of the separation of church and state. But, there is a mass of people out there who are really not of that opinion. The Constitution and laws concerning this matter do not intend to suppress religion, but declare the dangers of such a combination. A lot of people and maybe the majority of Americans have the perception that their religious belief or God's word is the ultimate authority over mankind. Whether this is the case or not, we mortals were given the options of choices, whether or not they respond to God's authority, regardless of the consequences. What the religious sector gives little thought to is that this is not a nation which was established only for Christians and Christian law.   If this were the case, our government would have a whole different look than it does today.

This country was established and the Constitution written by a group of people aware that the reason it even existed was primarily people getting away from countries which did not separate the church from state. How can one be so naive as to believe that the religious beliefs of the President or Congressmen should have authority over our government? For the well-meaning Christian movement who has these beliefs, can they not conceive the possibility of a religion of different beliefs having a member voted in as President or being the majority of Congressmen? If you throw religion into the political arena and any religious group has the ability to pass or sway legislation, we will have a big problem. If just the belief in God is the criteria there is less of a problem, but each secular group brings a lot of baggage with it. We have, Catholics, Mormons, Jews, Muslims, Protestants, Hindus, etc., who all believe in God, but when they are in control of a government and function under their religious influence, there will be a great difference in how the government will govern.

My perception of the people who run for political office and use religion as a talking point and claim that religion is a major part of their political philosophy, is that they are a danger to the foundation of this government. For years elected Presidents have governed without the undue influence of their religion. In the recent past and at the present and I assume in the future, religious beliefs are becoming more a part of the political philosophy of candidates.

Contrary to popular perception, the philosophy of *the majority rules* is not how it works in the U.S. We are 80% Christian, why don't we just pass laws based upon Christian principles? 90% of the people in this country do not believe in sport hunting, why don't we just eliminate it by vote? We are a country of laws which protect and respect the minority. Everyone in the U.S. is a minority in some fashion regardless of who they are or what they believe. My protection and your protection, as we are both a minority, is the standard of the U.S. We do not need a philosophy ruling our government that believes a religious belief supersedes the laws of the U.S. or even suggests it. We are all too aware of Sharia law, and we never want to get to that point.

Does religion have any place at all in our government? I don't see that it hurts anything as is, or has hurt anything in the past. Should they start the congressional sessions with a prayer? If it is not disruptive and does not interfere with the process, I see no harm in it, but prepare yourself for morning prayers. Should there be religious inscriptions on the walls or buildings, I see no harm in that either. This is a cultural matter, which reflects the history of the U.S. That will be my argument when an Atheist requests the same amount of time for his beliefs or wants to have all of the religious inscriptions removed. I would never argue from a point of religious belief, but always from a point of cultural history. Should we take *"In god we trust"* off our money? There is some idiot out there doing no more than stirring up a lot of unnecessary trouble. But, the answer to that as I perceive it is that, I don't know. We have millions of religious people upset and up in arms about this demand or proposal. I would like to ask these millions, does God even want his name stamped or printed on money, the root of all evil? Handled by drug dealers, prostitutes, corrupt governments and officials, thieves, murderers, and so on. Those of you who are sure he does, should continue your emotional opposition to its removal. The Atheists, who are demanding it, they should get a life.

As I have stated much earlier, a lot of people who have beliefs become brain locked into these beliefs and there is no negotiation, logic or evidence that will change their belief, regardless of the circumstances. Haven't we seen enough suicide bombers to recognize the danger? Of course this is just my perception of the separation of church and state. Do we want someone like this running the United States?

(32) Judges

Here I am writing about something I have had very little experience with personally. What little experience I have had and as well reading of court cases and judgements for fifty years I have a perception as to our system of judges. Our judges have way to much power over citizens or anything else as far as that goes. When in court a person can be abused, bullied, threatened and be at the mercy of the judge. This does not always happen, but the point is that they have the ability and right to do it if they so desire. I understand the judges position and job as the judge, but I question if many are totally impartial. In all likelihood, they did not get their position by being impartial.

The attorneys tell their clients what to do to please the judge and what not to do to piss him off.

(33) Being anal

This is a slang term that describes people that gripe other people to death due to their personality disorder. This disorder is exhibited by people who have to have everything a certain way when there is absolutely no good reason for it in the eyes of others. A perfect example of this which I have been forced to endure in the past is the person who has to have every pencil on his desk with the erasers in a perfect line and every pencil lined up by pencil length. Everything has to be in order and not the order that everyone else would desire, but their order. Being guilty of secretly repeatedly putting one of the pencils out of order by length, results in destroying the persons entire day and usually a tantrum.

Of course this behavior is not limited to pencils, but everything else in this person's world as well. Perfect order may seem to be an admirable trait, but it flies in the face of the shortest distance between two points is a straight line. This perfect order trait can destroy almost any business venture whether farming, construction or others. A perfectly straight irrigation line can cause one half the crops dying from lack of water.

This is a psychological problem so don't bother to try to convince these people that they are just simply anal, because they think everyone else is sloppy, lazy, irresponsible and unorganized.

(34) Domestic energy production

It has been my experience that the members of the public who object to the use of wind generators, have this objection on purely philosophical and political grounds. Their dislike for wind generators is based on statements such as; they are not reliable, expensive, not cost effective and so on. It is obvious to any rational listener that the real objection is that the resistance is being promoted by an opposing philosophy. They have no numbers to justify their position such as the actual reliability, cost and cost effectiveness, they just don't approve of them. Ask any U.S. citizen in opposition to wind generators about specific details as to power output, specifications, cost effectiveness, etc. and you will see a blank look on their face.

Even if they are not cost effective or price competitive, a lot of people have small generators for emergency situations and it is not irrational to believe as a matter of national security that our emergency power grid should have the same.

If anyone can prove to me that wind generators are not beneficial to the U.S., I will be the first to agree with them. The unacceptable thing to me is that some people have a negative perception of wind generators with little or no knowledge of them. They have been influenced by propaganda and whether the propaganda is right or wrong, they are not supposed to approve of them.

Nuclear power is perceived in the same manner. As for myself, nuclear power is absolutely fantastic until one of the nuclear power plants melts down. Do the benefits outweigh the risk? I guess it again is a matter of perception. Some say "Yes" and some say "No." Those saying "No" are looking at a worst case scenario of a meltdown whose effects could be absolutely devastating to the population and the environment of the U.S. The population in favor of nuclear power generation justifies it by downplaying the risk and the need for a clean power source. Again, both segments of the population are influenced by propaganda from opposing philosophical groups and not on facts and risk analysis. Even if the risk is acceptable, there is still that small risk of devastating proportion. Logic should make one conclude that if nuclear power is necessary for our power requirements, it should be eliminated as a power source as soon as it can be replaced with a safer method.

Solar power production is questionable to me because of its cost problems. Before I took it off of the table on philosophical grounds, I would at least be interested in its potential. Even if power production from solar was at a reasonable loss it could be beneficial. There is nothing beneficial about paying $4.00 a gallon for gasoline. How much of a loss are we taking there? I have researched solar panels, solar paint, solar shingles, solar furnaces, etc. The untapped energy source there is enormous. I am sure if we took the oil subsidies and tax breaks from the oil companies and gave them to the solar industry, we would see a great deal more interest from the private sector.

Then we have our domestic tar sands, oil sands, oil shale, gas deposits, coal deposits and a few others. We have energy deposits for centuries if we use them wisely. Assuming the scientists are correct and I would give them the benefit of the doubt over the private sector with vested interests, we have to clean up the pollutants created by using these power sources. If we could be self-sufficient due to fossil fuel production at a cost to the citizen at 25% higher than it is today due to this clean-up process, I am confident that in the long term we would greatly benefit the U.S. and as consumers we would come out ahead in the long run. As an example, if we paid $5.00 per gallon instead of $4.00 per gallon for gasoline, it would be a short-term hardship. We must get away from the public perception that gasoline will be $4.00 at a high and could go down to $3.50. The reality is that in the long term, under our present dependence from profit motivated and foreign sources, we will eventually see gasoline go to $5.00, $6.00, $7.00 and right on up. We will still be playing the same dumb catch up game with fuel economy cars until we are all driving motor scooters. Do we want to pay $5.00 per gallon from now on and eliminate a few wasteful trips and be able to breathe, or do we want to pay the $6.00, $7.00, $8.00, which will increase forever regardless of cleaning up the pollutants. Petroleum is not a renewable resource, which makes this a certainty.

Of course this will all require regulations by the U.S. government to maintain that $5.00 gasoline price because we will always have profit making entities that will strangle the consumer. One must also bear in mind that oil can be used as a weapon as easily as a bomb.

I have to keep repeating, that this is just my perception of the problems and solutions and I will change my perception if I am wrong or there is a better method available.

(35) Lobbyist and lobbying.

It is inconceivable to me that lobbying is a legal process. Fundamentally it is a situation whereby someone or some entity pays a lobbyist to influence the vote of a congressman or committee member. It is obvious to most that even though it is not illegal due to the Constitution, it should be. In some instances it is illegal depending upon the interpretation of lobbying as well as legislation passed by the same groups which receives funds from lobbyists. Lobbying in all of its various forms has been the cause of the most corruption of legislators and the reason for most of our dubious legislation. It is the major player in the philosophical war between political parties and political candidates. My perception of lobbying is; that it is, or is very near the bribery of public officials by special interest groups. At its best it is an unsavory practice.

Legislation has been passed in respect to lobbying, but be sure not to the extent that it will hinder the process.

(36) Environmentalists

Having operated a fairly large gold mining operation for a couple of years, I am fully aware of environmental laws and regulations. Today it is all but impossible to mine for any minerals in the U.S. except for gravel. Even these gravel pits are under strict regulation. There are several types of environmentalist and I will address my perception of these. Actually there are basically two types, those who have a basis for their beliefs and those who are going on belief alone.

The logical intent for any rational environmental regulations should be based upon damage done to biological life forms or damage done to other's property. An example of these would be if you were manufacturing and poisonous pollutants were released in a watershed or polluted the atmosphere with toxic emissions. Almost all existing environmental regulations are written to regulate a small source of environmental damage the same as a large source. There is a problem with this concept to the point that some regulations, I perceive as unjustifiable. Unjustifiable regulations that I am aware of are those which change the appearance of the landscape. Examples of these unjustified regulations are as examples; In Kansas in the early nineteen hundreds there was a lot of strip mining for coal going on. As there were no regulations at the time, the miners left hundreds of large pits in the ground. These pits filled with water and were left with piles of overburden around the pits. For decades after this, if you wanted to go fishing or squirrel hunting in Kansas, you would always head for the strip pits.

There was little fishing water in Kansas other than these pits and the overburden piles were tree covered and alive with squirrels and other wildlife. Well, due to environmental regulations, these pits were filled in and the pits were lost forever as an area of entertainment.

In the western states there are many locations where gold dredges left huge piles of rocks and small ponds, cottonwood trees and swampy areas. Surrounding these areas is flat poor grade pastureland for miles. There are environmentalists who think the mined areas are a real eyesore. I do not understand what is so appealing or interesting about a flat cow pasture and cow pies, but it would be near impossible today to disturb a cow pasture by placer mining. Also, putting extremely mildly dirty water into a river that runs mud several months a year is also pretty costly if you are caught, to like $30,000.00 per day. I was caught and had to plea for mercy and make some deals with the State to get out of that situation.

But in all things, there is room for thought. Which brings me to some philosophical arguments and thoughts in respect to the environment.. Do humans have the right to bring any other life form to extinction and have a good argument against environmental regulations preventing this? From my own personal perspective, I think not. If you are a Creationist, it would seem somewhat foolhardy to eliminate a specie that was created for this Earth. If not a Creationist, what you must consider is that it took millions of years of struggling to survive by a species and we eliminate that millions of years struggle, probably so we can make some money and piss it away on beer and beef jerky.

Because we are more intelligent and have the means to kill any other creature or entire species on earth, including ourselves, do we have the right? It has been my perception that the people that I know who believe that we do, have an unrealistic admiration for the human species. We will eventually destroy the human species unless nature or divine forces do it for us, and what biological organisms we leave will rule the Earth. History has shown that we have been slaughtering *each other* for thousands of years, so why would one not expect someone to shoot the last snow leopard. The snow leopard should not expect any more mercy than we show each other, or sixty million bison.

I guess the bottom line on environmental issues is that we are better off with environmental regulations than without them. With them, we can't do anything, and without them there won't be anything. As for me, if I am starving to death I will eat the last spotted owl on Earth, but if I am not, I will definitely not eliminate it. If it were not for early environmentalists like Teddy Roosevelt, we wouldn't have any wildlife or national parks today.

(37) Largemouth bass fishing

I have seen so many bass fishing programs on television that I have it down to about one microsecond to change channels when I encounter one. I have fished the better part of my life away and I have caught a lot of largemouth bass. I enjoyed catching a bass now and then, *but my God*. It is very obvious that we have a bass fishing culture out there in great numbers. For years I have watched bass fishermen in their bass boats flogging the water. They all do the same thing in the same spots. A boat leaves and another shows up at the same location and does the same thing and then races away at seventy miles per hour in the bass boat. I have listened to TV programs and read articles about every conceivable aspect of bass fishing. The water temperature, the water clarity, the Ph of the water, the 1000 different best lures developed every year, depth finders, trolling motors, best bass boats, underwater structure, presentation, lines, poles, pre-fishing, tournament tours, Bass Masters, etc, etc.. My God, they are fishing for a muddy water fish that will bite anything and doesn't fight worth a damn and using 50# test line on a one pound fish. Then to top it off there is Bill Dance in his boat on that obvious private lake catching obviously stocked big largemouth every cast and I have to listen to the secrets of bass fishing. My perception of the issue is that these people live where all there is to catch is bass or they have never fished for anything else. Unless of course there is a *buck* to be made.

So as not to completely alienate myself from the bass fishing culture, the bass fishermen can at least make fun of the walleye fishermen. And probably the worst case scenario is myself, who has spent thousands of hour fishing and I don't even eat fish.

(38) Love and sex

These are two topics which are perceived by some people as one being a prerequisite for the other, and not necessarily in the order I gave them. Love, as we humans understand it is a random deep emotional attraction of one individual towards another. This attraction is more similar to a drug addiction than most people would like to believe. The same portion of the brain that is responsible for the love of cocaine is responsible for the love towards another human. Whereas the experienced euphoria of cocaine is forced upon the brain until it loves it, this is not the case with human attractions. Love and having an affair with someone are usually two different things. An affair satisfies one portion of the brain, but not the portion responsible for the love attraction. Human beings like some other mammals have a desire to stay with another specific individual for an extended period. This is obviously not always the case in our society, but the tendency is still there. The original passionate love attraction, over time, seems to change in nature or in some cases just disappears altogether. The numbers of cases where it remains and the cases where it disappears are both a good percentage of the people and for this reason divorces usually occur in a situation where there is one way love.

The portion of the brain which possesses this love attraction can be so obsessed by it that there are extensive lengths a person will go to satisfy this attraction. Millions of lives have been lost due to the love attraction of some and in many cases if this love attraction cannot be satisfied, the brain will physically eliminate itself in a suicide event.

There is a very good reason for humans having this portion of their brain allocated for the love attraction. This reason, simply being for the propagation of the specie and the rearing of the newborn. As the portion of the brain responsible for the sex drive in humans more or less works best in conjunction with the love portion, it is not at all absolutely necessary. The sex drive portion is the absolute drive for propagation, whereas the love portion creates a social setting possible for newborns to be cared for.

One only has to look to other mammals and their means of propagation of their specie. Their process seems to vary greatly and all seem to be different than humans, which I perceive is due to our intellect and consciousness of ourselves, as well as the long dependency of human children.

In most mammals there is no indication there is anything but a sex drive propagating their specie. In some others, there appears to be a recognition of their sex partners, which goes beyond the sex act and then just leaving the scene.

In respect to love and sex, there is an extremely interesting aspect of selecting mates. If you are a female elk, you are just a captive audience, but still you will be bred by the biggest, strongest guy in town. But in some cases of mammals and in humans, the selection process is quite distinct. In the case of other living creatures, there are sexes who are attracted to something, and there are those who are just attractive. In the animal world, usually the males are brightly colored or perform embarrassing actions to attract a mate who is looking for the most colorful or the most strange or embarrassing behavior. We have to give the peacock an "A" for colorful in this respect. Male frogs chirp and bellow, male birds build fancy nests, and the list goes on and on to include every animal on Earth.

Are humans any different? Yes and no. Every human will participate in this process, but our longevity and our self-consciousness makes the process somewhat different.

Human males are attracted to all females to varying degrees, but their brain does not always necessarily make a selection as to love partners. There are appearances and qualities that the brain picks up on when making its love selection. In most cases the selection process is not instantaneous by design. It would do a normal male little good to fall instantly in love with Miss America and the brain acknowledges this. Somehow it sets limits for itself as to the possibilities. The female brain seems to be more selective yet, which explains millions of males running around making fools of themselves.

Correct me if I am wrong, but my perception of the situation is that males are driven primarily by the appearance of females and everything else falls behind that. Rich billionaires will fall madly in love with servants, barmaids, spies, etc., regardless of their status, which is trumped by appearance.

Females on the other hand seem more likely to fall in love with what a male brings to the table, rather than appearance. The high school quarterback, the doctor, the fancy car, their money, their notoriety, etc, and then lastly their appearance. Not that they don't actually fall in love with the guy, but there are prerequisites. You see very few males of wealth, notoriety, position, or own a Rolls Royce that there is not a good-looking wife hanging on his arm. It works out well for both as their attractions are satisfied. Now for us ugly, unsuccessful people, we have to fake it a lot with shiny things we can't afford and a lot of lipstick and makeup.

(39) Pets and health

There have been many studies that have proven that having a pet, for most people will lower their blood pressure when they are in the vicinity of their pet.

That is the good news.

The bad news is that when in the vicinity of the same pet, everyone else's blood pressure increases. The barking pet dog in the back yard may have a soothing effect on the owners, but everyone else in earshot is about ready to lose it.

The interesting aspect of all of this is that we have one or two people who are going to live to be a hundred and dozens who are going to die early on from high blood pressure.

I have no evidence to support my perception, but I reluctantly believe this phenomenon could easily be expanded to include other people's kids as well.

(40) The holidays

Do we actually enjoy the Thanksgiving, Christmas and New Year's Day holidays?

Speaking only for myself and those who dare not admit it, we don't. The total confusion and stress starts before Thanksgiving and endures through New Year's Day. The aspect of the onrushing holidays stresses me at the mere thought of it.

Of course this is a time of family gatherings. These holidays bring out the best and the worst of stressful situations due to what is required to celebrate them and all of the different personalities thrown in close proximity to each other. I will just list some of the things that have to be considered or accomplished and if it does not give you the cold chills you are in a coma.

Where will everybody gather on these days? Who will do the cooking? What will we bring for dinner? We have to buy and send dozens of cards. How many family members will there be? Be sure and take the camera. What am I going to buy for presents that are just what they want? Who is going to set up the table? Do we eat at the table and where are the others going to eat? Is everybody on time after anticipating the dinner for nine months? No. Is there a constant stream of people entering and leaving the house and a discussion about every arrival and departure? How many might be able to make it? What time should we eat? Are we going to come back later for leftovers? Who is going to clean up the dinner mess? Are there going to be girlfriends or boyfriends? Who is going to clean up the kitchen again? This year it's going to be different, but it never is.

I could go on forever.

(41) Congress and congressmen.

I have received countless emails in respect to congressmen and their benefits. 95% of these emails were in error as to the content and the sender knew they were, or did not know they were, and I don't know which is worse. The emails explained congressmen's wages, health benefits, pensions, housing, health care plans and on and on. I researched these erroneous allegations and it was actually quite interesting. Somewhat complex, but my perception of what I had researched was that as compared to the private sector, the wages and benefits are extraordinarily low.

I asked myself, this being the case, why would a person spend an enormous amount of time and a great deal of his money as well as others on a chance of getting the job? In some cases we are talking millions to get elected to the job. The wages and benefits are absolutely no incentive, so there must be an answer. If one can determine the answer he may be able to understand that there is definitely something wrong here and what it is. If not for the money and benefits, what? I have given the possibilities I think require consideration and my thoughts are; Although the wages and benefits are not worth the time and effort, there may be ways to personally enrich one's self due to the job title and the functions of a Congressman. Another obvious possibility is that you do not need benefits or more money, you do it for self-satisfaction as you have little else to do. An ego trip is also good candidate. You enjoy the notoriety and the social aspects of it all. You desire the admiration and respect of other people and subordinates. You want to be recognized by the leaders of this country and rub shoulders with them. You enjoy the game of it all. You are trying to facilitate a political agenda.

There are many other reasons of course, but at the very bottom of this list is that you spend the time and effort as well as the social inconvenience, to represent every one of your constituents for the benefit of them. This may sound somewhat cynical, but I have a hard time seeing a person totally disrupting his family life as well as his present occupation, spending a lot of time on the road, living out of state, for a position that pays little and may last as few as two years for the purpose of just doing what he is told by his constituents.

It is possibly that it is all of the above, as that is the nature of the job they are taking on.

(42) Unforgotten memories

There is a perception by people that their memory is limited to significant events and the older they get the more significant the event has to be or it is lost. I am sure dying brain cells take a lot of information with them, but I contend that there are thousands of memories which just can't be brought back up to the conscious level and some that can.

Under hypnosis people often remember things which are impossible when they are conscious. There is a little mind game I play on rare occasion, which to some degree makes my point. The game is to try to remember the most insignificant thing that I have experienced or observed. The hardest examples are in the more distant past. These are things that for the rest of your life you would never think of.

It could be a beer bottle along the side of the road forty years ago or a small rock you saw in a BestBuy planter ten years ago while waiting for the wife. I warn that this is a very stressful game and requires 100% concentration, but the results are well worth the effort. It is self-satisfying that you have not lost all of the past. I would guess that people in solitary confinement are well aware of this little game.

(43) American history

American history as taught and perceived by most Americans as compared to reality is really not the same thing. For patriotic reasons if nothing else, the highlights of American history and the players, have been gleaned, written about and taught. The actual historic events as they took place, the actions of individuals and the personalities of individuals have been ignored. Most of this has been documented and is available to the public, but you would have to have great deal of interest to find the information, or even care to.

As perceived, somehow a large group of super intellects appeared from out of the woodwork and established this nation. The Declaration of Independence and the Bill of Rights is proof of this perception of their super intellect as the American public revere it as being above the current capacity of our citizenry. They are the last word and our government and society is ruled by these documents. The reality of the situation is that our founding fathers, although many were intellects, were a disorganized, confrontational group of the higher-class citizens at the time. The idea to secede from the British colonies was perceived by many of our forefathers as ridiculous and they felt it was not in the best interest of themselves or the states/colonies they represented. This was not a case where a group of people arrived to declare their support and sign a document. It was comparable to a dogfight. Some had little to lose and all of them had their lives to lose.

After declaring independence you would have to fight for it. The English were not just going to walk away from their vested interest.

The history of each signer of the Declaration of Independence is easily available, and it isn't necessarily that inspiring. The Revolutionary War was continuing at the time and things were not going well for the army. It could and very nearly was a disaster when time came to defend the newly established U.S. government.

The character and lifestyles of our forefathers involved, ran the gauntlet from statesmen and States representatives to men of social and lifestyle background which was questionable. As an example, Thomas Jefferson was a slaveholder and fathered mixed race children by a black servant, while living with his wife and children on his property. By today's standards, this may be unacceptable, but at the time it was not out of the ordinary or illegal. Ben Franklin was known internationally as a playboy, and George Washington eventually made a living making more whiskey than anyone else in the U.S. And these were the three great patriots of the time. Lord only knows what the lesser group was involved in

I don't have a problem with any of these endeavors, as that was then and this is now. It was also not clearly defined at the time of debating our independence from Britain, whether we would have a President or a Monarch.

The bottom line is that it was definitely not a simple gathering of like-minded patriots with a grand design. The

Declaration of Independence and The Bill of Rights was very controversial at the time as they were not agreeable to everyone. They had to be changed due to circumstances that prevailed at the time.

The wording of the original Bill of Rights and quotes from those involved in the entire independence movement might be quite troublesome to some today. Some readers may have heard of the Federalist Papers which were produced later by some involved which explained what they really thought.

This misconception of our forefathers has left the people today with an attitude, which may be a good thing. Just one example of a quote by Abraham Lincoln represents my thoughts on the misconception of American History.

"I will say then that I am not, nor ever have been in favor of bringing about in anyway the social and political equality of the white and black races - that I am not nor ever have been in favor of making voters or jurors of negroes, nor of qualifying them to hold office, nor to intermarry with white people; and I will say in addition to this that there is a physical difference between the white and black races which I believe will forever forbid the two races living together on terms of social and political equality. And inasmuch as they cannot so live, while they do remain together there must be the position of superior and inferior, and I as much as any other man am in favor of having the superior position assigned to the white race. I say upon this occasion I do not perceive that because the white man is to have the superior position the negro should be denied everything." -- September 18, 1858 - Fourth Debate with Stephen A. Douglas at Charleston, Illinois

Throughout the history of the U.S. there is not a great deal of knowledge of, or interest in, how we as a nation started with a very small portion of North America and eventually ended up with the borders we have today. This was probably jammed into a one-hour history class in high school.

It is an intriguing story. A lot of the story is not a pretty one and there are some moral issues involved. For the most part, we bullied our way from coast to coast. As we all know, when the colonists arrived in this country it was highly populated by aboriginal people. For the most part the concept of land ownership was an unheard of concept to these people. Land space controlled by various tribes was on the other hand a very important issue. This being the case, the land space controlled by the various tribes was usually concluded by confrontation and therefore changed frequently.

We introduced the concept of land ownership to the natives and bargained for it at very reasonable rates because they were land rich and technology poor. A steel hatchet was worth a great deal of land that a Native American could easily do without. Of course there were also large vacant areas available thanks to the diseases we unwittingly and unwillingly passed on to them.

Who would have thought that Napoleon would be responsible for our acquisition of Middle America? Our acquisition of the southwest and the west I will discuss later, but it was under questionable circumstances. We purchased Alaska and acquired the Hawaiian Islands to make us complete.

Congress was of course involved in all of this, which required a vote to pass the bill or legislation. Of all of the many positive social issues and acquisition of property which were an unbelievably good deal, it is amazing that the bills or laws making this possible were very nearly voted down by members of Congress. Of course while the Congress was acquiring resources, they were giving them away at the same time. It makes one wonder, what in the hell were these people thinking, but then we are wondering the same thing about Congress today. Congressmen seem incapable of functioning in the best interest of every citizen in the United States. They function in the best interest of groups of people in the United States. These could be labor unions, liberals, conservatives, Democrats, Republicans, Wall Street, the oil interests, private enterprise, the military and many other groups. These groups evolved with the history of the U.S. and have lobbied and manipulated congress since day one.

Regardless of all of the shortcomings and historical lack of foresight by Congress, we are still here, and that is more than a lot of other international governments can say. To close the issue of the misconception of U.S. history, I can only say that we can be proud of what we have accomplished, but do not look at our history and the players through rose colored glasses. Our pride should be tempered with a lot of humility and we should not be overly critical of other country's histories and their players as we risk being hypocrites.

There is a subject which could well be discussed in several of the other topics in this book, but I will address it as a U.S. history event.

The U.S. has experienced a social phenomenon which was established in 1866. This phenomenon gave itself the title Ku Klux Klan.

Everyone in the U.S. has good reason to suppress discussion of it's existence, which has been for the last 150 years. Its existence and actions is likened to a mentally handicapped child decades ago who was hidden in a room of the house and not made aware of by the community.

The period of time I am most aware of is from about 1920 on. Fundamentally, the Ku Klux Klan has always consisted of a group of like-minded people with a philosophy based upon hate. This hate may have been justifiable by a few, but it is beyond reason that it was justifiable by all of the members involved. The Klan started out as a small group and at its peak had an inconceivable membership of well over two million members. The foundation of this organization was hate for other groups of people residing in the U.S. The groups were primarily the African-Americans, Jews and Catholics or anyone associated with them. The unmistakable identification of this organization was the white robe and hood (another secret society) they wore as well as the huge wood crosses they burned in ceremonies. The average Caucasian American has little knowledge as to the impact this organization had on American society from 1920 through 1970.

The Klan used the principle which we now refer to as terrorism to pursue its philosophy. At its most prominence, the Klan had infiltrated and had members in almost every position in the local, state and Federal Government and was a large voting block.

The Klan has diminished in size to a few thousand members due to the efforts of the Federal Government during the middle twentieth century.

I like everyone else will not dwell on this subject as no good can come from it. I would like to say that the Klan was predominantly Christian and had a predominant political affiliation, which I will not address because that was then, and this is now. For the most part the Klan is gone, but one may detect beliefs and philosophies lingering around which are similar in nature to the Klan philosophy.

This brings to my mind the subject of Roman history, which is very interesting. If it were not for movies, Americans would have little knowledge of it. Our misconception of our history being only of short duration as compared to the Romans, reminds me of a book which was made into a 13 part TV series titled *I Claudius*. Claudius was an Emperor of Rome who intentionally left the Emperorship to Nero, after he Claudius, was poisoned. He knew that Nero would destroy Rome and that was acceptable to him. The story is based on factual people and events and is the biography of Claudius. At a point late in his life, Claudius secretly wrote of his life in Rome and the total corruption, bloodlust and ruthlessness of the leaders of Rome. When his autobiography was complete, he made a copy that he knew would be found and destroyed after his death. The original was hidden, to be found thousands of years later. What was the reason for this biography? Well, Claudius was certain that in the distant future, people would never believe or be taught of the atrocities committed and they would probably never even hear of them.

Our country's history is nothing like the atrocious Roman history, but the concept is the same. If our shortcomings and misdeeds as a nation are not documented and available to citizens, we have a tendency to become somewhat self-righteous, which is obvious to some of our neighboring countries. We learn by mistakes, but we need to know what the mistakes were.

If we are going to be the greatest nation on Earth, we have to give our actions a lot of thought and stay on our toes to maintain that status. To be the greatest nation on Earth, other countries must fear your wrath, but your wrath must be based on the highest moral principles. The U.S. must have the respect of the rest of the world.

(44) One World Order

For years I have been hearing conspiracy theories about *One World Order* and the people and organizations instigating this worldwide governing power. My perception of One World Order is that it is an insinuation and accusation made to describe anyone or any endeavor which indicates cooperation between more than two countries and usually pertains to money. The establishment of the Euro is a good example and the One World Order was spouted continuously by the factions opposing the Euro. The world trade organization is another example of the supposed One World Order. It is a political tool used by both liberals and conservatives as they see fit to oppose specific international agreements. In reality it is my perception that the One World Order is a myth. It is a myth in that it will never happen. Some philosopher may have toyed with the idea, but in the real world it is not a possibility, as some individuals perceive it. The perception being that in cooperation with each other, countries or groups in power in different countries, will voluntarily form a one-world government. It is not absolutely impossible, but the only context in which this could happen and sustain itself is if the groups were all of a particular religious faith. Religions have in the past brought human social behavior and growth to a crawl for hundreds of years, so this theory has some merit. The Muslim religion as taught is entirely in favor of a One-World Order, under the direction of God and the Muslims. I don't foresee a time when everyone on the earth is Muslim unless the people of all other faiths are all dead.

A One World Order with the populations and beliefs of all of the citizens on Earth, will not work because there is not even a single population of any country on Earth that is controllable. Every country has social problems resulting in violence, crime and political disputes. Can you imagine combining all of these populations under one ruling faction? It would require a police state that would immediately be overthrown. People who are honestly concerned about a One World Order could better spend their time worrying about a One Country Order in this country, which is entirely possible where over 80% of the citizens are of one religious belief. If this happens, prepare yourself for another couple hundred years of no social or economic development. The Mennonites are an example of a religious society that can stay locked in time. It will be a while before you see a Mennonite space ship.

(45) Genetically engineered crops.

There is a lot of controversy in respect to genetically engineered crops. I really don't understand why there is a controversy, but it is hinted that there may be a safety factor involved. My perception of genetically engineered crops is that they will not be a public safety problem. To my knowledge, there are few to no crops that we eat worldwide that have not been genetically engineered either by nature or farmers for the last thousands of years. Almost all of the vegetables that we eat today were at one time not edible or barely edible. Our ancestors familiar with foods such as, bananas, melons, carrots, corn, tomatoes, cabbage and almost every other edible plant, would tell us that the plants were almost unrecognizable as to what we have today. This was all done by humans selectively breeding, cross-pollinating, hybrids and I suppose other methods. These crops were engineered into a variation of the original. To my knowledge none of this created a health issue. There is a chance that a person of religious persuasion thinks that we are changing God's grand design. This may be the case, but if there were a lot of delicious vegetables in the Garden of Eden, they were left there. Adam and Eve were thrown into the wilderness with less desirable plants and if their decedents were to survive they had to cope with this problem.

There is a possibility that I consider may exist when genetically engineering plants. Every plant on Earth has a genetic defense system. The basis for this is that all plants or portions of them are poisonous or have a repellent to insects. A cherry fly maggot will never be found in an apple, or an apple maggot in a cherry. Although all plants have this genetic defense, a few insects have evolved or cracked the code so that they can flourish on a particular plant and usually only that one. There are plants that are poisonous to animals regardless of the insect issue. Logic would tell you that the reason for this is so that they do not get eaten by animals. On a same poisonous plant which includes fruit, the fruit almost always is not poisonous to animals and in fact it is quite tasty to animals. Simply, the plant wants animals to eat the fruit containing seeds and disperse them, usually away from the plant. This makes everybody happy and propagates the plant specie.

My concern, which may not be warranted, is that during the genetic engineering of a plant species, the genes which determine the toxic trait of a plant may be altered or interfered with so that toxins may now be in the fruit as well as the plant. It would seem to me that this could quickly be determined by testing and laboratory animal test.

(46) Radiation

Radiation is a lot like electricity. Most scientists know what it is, but few really completely understand it or explain it to us average people.

The people who work around it, who are not scientists, have less of an idea. I have worked around radiation and with radioisotopes for 30 years and unlike Sarah Palin, I don't think radiation is good for you.

For the most part, the American citizens are completely ignorant of radioisotopes, radiation, the types of radiation, and the effects of radiation on the human body. My perception is that there is no safe amount of radiation which is absorbed by the human body.

The human body contends with radiation every day and has some defenses against it. We have radiation from the Sun which we are absorbing every day and is of most concern to people who are flying high in the atmosphere a great deal of the time. The atmosphere absorbs a great deal of the radiation and at sea level or shielded from this radiation it is of little concern, but possibly could still have an effect on a human cell. Now direct sunlight, which is a form of radiation the average citizen is aware of, is much more severe. We humans walk around in the sunlight every day with a misconception of just how dangerous and lethal it is. In direct overhead unobstructed sunlight, an unprotected

Caucasian human can absorb it only hours before the radiation has so severely damaged the skin tissue that hospitalization or death could occur. Extended periods are certain death. All of us have experienced what we call sunburn and can relate to how short a period of time this takes. That is in the short term, but exposure to sunlight being a form of radiation, is a major cause of skin cancer due to damage to cell components. Radiation easily kills or damages human cells. The human body has a defense against normal amounts of radiation or there would not be any humans around today. Humans with dark skin coloring are not affected a great deal by the damaging effects of sunlight to the skin (of which I have very limited knowledge) and those in areas of consistent sunlight people tend to be tall and lean so as to limit their body's surface area to the sun. With a head of hair, they tend to stand in their own shadow. I have read that in the northern latitudes people are built as to have more surface area to absorb the warmth of the sun as well as to insulate the heat they generate themselves. Another defense against the normal amount of natural radiation is that the human body replenishes dead cells in most tissue. In the tissue that does not reproduce, the sheer number of cells in the tissue can tolerate the loss of a few.

Man-made radiation and the doses that can be received is another matter. The amount of man-made radiation absorbed by the body is potentially astronomical as compared to natural occurring radiation. As well, now we are talking about contaminating radiation. Absorbed contaminating radiation is potentially a death sentence. This depends upon the type radiation, the half-life, the radioisotope and the normal or medically induced functions of the body to pass the radioisotope out of the body. Contaminating radiation is bad news. Exposure to gamma ray radiation such as x-rays is different in that the damage is done only during the exposure. A lot of the radiation passes completely through the human body depending upon the wavelength of the radiation, but that which does not pass through is absorbed by cells in the human body and they are; not significantly damaged, severely damaged or conceivably genetically altered.

None of this is good. My perception of the medical use of radiation is that the general public is misinformed or not informed about the damage to the human body by x-rays. If the topic arises, the argument for the medical use of radiation is that it is a tradeoff for the benefit of being able to diagnose or heal a more dangerous condition. In some cases this is true and in some cases it is not. Knowing the damage to the human body, I have probably had as may x-rays as anyone, as well as being exposed to the industrial use of gamma rays for 30 years. As far as the industrial exposure, blue-collar workers are used to life threatening conditions in the workplace and accept that. When I have a medical x-ray, I just write off a few hundred thousand cells and potentially a certain length of time of my life, to potentially detect something that is going to kill me next week. I have real concern about the use of dental x-rays as I don't have that many functioning brain cells anyway and these don't reproduce. In closing I would just say that the less radiation you are exposed to the better off you are.

The general public should be completely informed about medical x-rays and the excessive use of x-rays should be a criminal offense due to the damage incurred by the human body.

(47) Secret societies in the U.S.

Probably the two best known secret societies in the U.S. are the Masons and the Skull and Bones Society. The Masons have been around since the founding of this country and the Skull and Bones Society not much later.

The term secret society implies that there is a society, which is supposed to be unknown to all of the rest of society. As this is impossible, their beliefs and actions are the secret. The Masons have been around forever and the public attention given them has pretty well revealed everything there is possible to learn of their beliefs and actions. Exactly what role they had in the establishment of this nation is not clear, but it is obvious that they played a major role. A lot of our founding fathers were Masons, which was at the time a secret society. Conspiracy theories abound as to their intent. If one is content with the history of the U.S., they could conclude that the Masonic influence was a good thing. If one looks at all of the historic Masonic artifacts left as structures or designs, he could as well conclude that there was and is a Masonic conspiracy, but to what end one can only speculate. One World Order? Whatever the case, there is little evidence that the conspiracy is having an effect upon the U.S. other than by promoting more conspiracy theories.

The Skull and Bones Society is a much more secret society as it is newer, smaller, and less publicized. It is a society limited to the Yale fraternity. The most popular people who have been, or still are members, are George H. W. Bush, John Kerry and George W. Bush. It is possible to obtain a list of people who have belonged to this society and the positions they have held in the U.S. government and the private sector.

My perception of secret societies and the U.S. government is such that I wonder why any rational person would vote for someone who belongs to a secret society. What is the secret? Are they planning to destroy the U.S. government? Are they trying to control the money in the U.S.? Do they plan on establishing a new government? Are they trying to establish a New World order? Just what insidious secret or plans do they have that 99.99% of the population of the U.S. cannot know about? If 99.99% of the population will not be told of the secret, you can be pretty certain there is a reason for that and it is obviously something they don't want us to hear.

We don't know what the secret is and it may not be any of the above, but then again it might. Voting for these people without the knowledge of their intent is not saying much for the rational intellect of a voter. One can excuse those who are not aware of these peoples affiliation with the secret society. The three individuals I have noted above have been questioned as to the Skull and Bones Society and they publicly and privately refuse to answer any questions about the society. This is on National TV, and still they receive votes by the millions to become Presidents or Congressmen. What does that say for the American voters who voted for them? I have heard the term, blind allegiance and I guess this is a classic example of that. This being the case, why would any rational person be influenced by one of these people who vote for members of a secret society?

Having read extensively about the Masons and the Skull and Bones Society and their members and their public and private achievements in our society, I have arrived at a perception of both. These perceptions may be incorrect, but it is how I perceive them with the information I have accumulated.

The Masons have philosophical beliefs in the structure of international society. Some of these beliefs are supernatural in nature and some are in respect to what one could say is One World Order. They also intend to be deeply involved in the domestic actions of individual citizens in respect to their behavior. They are very ritual orientated as witnessed by any of the functions they attend such as funerals and religion does not appear to be an integral part of these rituals.

The Skull and Bones Society as I understand it is completely different in their beliefs, and their intent is much simpler. My perception of this society is that it is a society comprised of people who have power or money or the potential to be powerful and wealthy. Research indicates that members of the Skull and Bones Society, later in life become the rich and powerful if they are not already. This is attained through the combined efforts of all of the other members. The membership is restricted to those who will be destined for power and wealth. The society has been quite successful if you examine the positions and wealth the members have obtained. There are some reported distasteful rituals involved in being a member of the society and it is not clear what their purpose is unless it is to test the resolve of the members. This is truly a secret society in that the members refuse to discuss it. There is no evidence of unlawful conduct other than stealing an Indian skull and I don't know the resolution of that matter. John Kerry or George W. Bush could explain the actions of all of the past society members, but they refuse to do that.

If my perception of the society is correct, members have been elected President of the United States and have been appointed to many government positions by government officials as well as being positioned in the highest ranks of the private sector. The bottom line is that this organization is the ultimate in cronyism.

This in every case may be perfectly legal or it may not be. In the case of politics in this country it surely has an impact upon our democracy. If not illegal, it gives certain people an unfair advantage and possibly a group of dozens is determining the leaders and policies of the United States. In the case of George W bush, he may have been tapped for the society due to his potential as merely being a Bush. Apparently the society had its reservation because his given society nickname was *Temporary*. All Skull and Bones members are designated a society nickname.

A political party may see the advantage in selecting a society member to run for office because they are aware of the power of the society in achieving success for their members.   The ordinary citizen may have heard of the society and brushed it off as an insignificant college fraternity thing, whereas the more powerful and wealthy in this country are well aware of what it really is.

The issue in my eyes is, how could a person vote for a candidate who refuses to tell them the intent of the secret society to which he belongs? The intent could be anything. President Obama had to contend with the prospect of impeachment because he would not prove unsubstantiated rumors, such as that he was really a Muslim and not an American citizen. The worst case scenario would be that this was true and we already knew what the secret was. In the case scenario of the Skull and Bones Society and government officials who belong to it, we have no idea, and what the worst case scenario could be. Reaching into the field of conspiracies, the members of the society may be afraid of the consequences of explaining the intent of the society.

(48) Philosophy

Philosophy is the study of human conditions and is to be satisfied by rational argument. If one has a particular philosophical belief, to his satisfaction it has been proven by rational argument or some may declare *common sense,* indicating that humans in common, make sense of the position.

One of many problems with philosophical beliefs is that most rational arguments satisfying a belief is done on an individual basis and was not open to argument by others. Or, a person recognizes that someone has already performed the rational argument and this person tells him the conclusion of the rational argument. This conclusion to be passed on to other people as the rational answers to a wide variety of topics. Americans are not very astute philosophers. This requires a lot of rational thought and rational thought may lead them to an unacceptable conclusion. For this reason, they don't even want to go there. We do not want to use rational arguments because it is too messy and usually requires a few people capable of rational thought to argue the matter. Regrettably we live in a society where there is only one side to every story. Proof of this is the popularity of individuals and networks who contend that they have done the rational argument; and they are *always bias* towards a specific agenda. That is plenty good enough for the masses listening because they have rationally had the argument with themselves and arrived at the same conclusion. In reality, most people are wrong most of the time and that is why I question how I perceive things. I feel I have a different perspective than a lot of people because I refuse to be brain locked to any philosophical position. If there is a rational argument that disproves any of my perceptions of things, I will accept that argument. Then I wonder if the human brain is capable of rational arguments on a lot of topics.

I also wonder if there are a lot of topics that there is no rational argument for. The primitive elements of the human brain may override rational behavior or arguments. You see people doing irrational things every day. If their brain was using rational thought, they would not be doing irrational things. If this is the case, we are in deep trouble as a specie; but then again we **are** in deep trouble, aren't we? An Albert Einstein quote: "The thing that drives me hazy, is it me or is everyone else crazy." I would think that there is not a human on Earth, not asking that question. The reason there are no more great philosophers is that it doesn't pay worth a damn and no one listens to them anyway. It is similar to poets and poetry in this respect. If you watch Congress in action, it is obvious that everyone has already arrived at a conclusion and committed their vote before the rational arguments begin. So much for Philosophy and rational argument.

(49) The brain

My knowledge, understanding and perception of the human brain, complicates but explains, at least to me, my perception of the actions of humans. My perception of the human brain is that it is the master of the body that it is in.

All other organs or physical components are there just to transport the brain to where it wants to be and react to the commands of the brain. Historically, for reasons I understand to some degree, there has been given a lot of importance given to the heart organ as a portion of the human body which seems to have some importance in respect to human behavior. Behaviors such as love, compassion, remorse and so forth have been associated with the heart. This is incorrect of course as these are all functions of the brain, but the heart is the only organ that consistently can be felt beating and can be heard. It is not hard to imagine then that people would attach significance to it.

My perception of the human brain is that it is essentially a highly sophisticated biological computer. It performs functions like all modern computers as to calculations and operating remote devices. It has audio and visual capabilities and reacts to all the sensory organs of the body and it has massive storage capacity for data from the environment around it. The brain analyses all of this data and reacts to it or just stores it for future use. The human brain is a marvel in its capacity for storing data. Unbelievably there are a few people who can recall almost every day of their lives. From my less capable brain, I have concluded that almost all of this data is stored as visual images. The human brain is compartmentally organized. Certain easily defined portions of the brain perform different functions, but all work in conjunction with each other. The vast and unbelievable ability of trillions of cells working in unison requires an unimaginable complexity.

My perception and understanding of the human brain is essential to my understanding of the nature of human beings and my questions about the actions of humans.

All human brains are not created equal. This miracle of nature is vulnerable to thousands of different biological and data processing defects. Most of these fundamental defects are genetically inherited traits, problems during gestation, the environment or chemical substances can cause a lot of them. Some are very common such as Down Syndrome, while some just randomly occur during the gestation period when the brain is growing and developing. Although all brains are the same, as they are brains, every brain is different. Every brain has different abilities and a lot of this is due to hereditary traits. Some brains have the ability to store more data, process the data faster and better and have superior inherent abilities such as artistic abilities. This difference in a brain's abilities runs from very poor to very good. We all fit in there somewhere and it has been my experience that each brain can usually detect the brains walking around that are superior or inferior.

What is called mental illness is the malfunctioning condition of a noticeable number of human brains being carried around. There are countless varieties of mental illness ranging from barely noticeable to severe.

Now for the mentally competent brains, which hopefully make up the majority of humans, we are encountered with the problems of a normal human brain. There are portions of these normal brains that the conscious brain has no control over. These are portions of the brain which instantly react to environmental stimuli and also constitute something I will call inherent character. Some human babies are crying at birth and cry for no apparent reason. Other babies just lie there and slobber and look around and they call these good babies. Some sleep and then cry, sleep and then cry, while the others sleep all night. This is what I call inherent character and seems to continue with these individuals their entire life. This could well be characteristics of our Type A and Type B personalities.

In addition to this malady we have with normal brains, we are confronted with the problems which all normal brains have. Even as miraculous as the brain is and all of its abilities, the human brain is unbelievably easy to manipulate. The brain is easily hypnotized and people think they are chickens or pigs. There are multitudes of visual deceptions which the brain cannot figure out. The brain is easily, what is called brainwashed. The brain can be led to believe almost anything. It just has to initially be programmed that what it hears is the truth. The brain is very susceptible to this procedure and will even help with the process. Whatever this belief may be, the brain will rationalize all future data it receives as a bias towards this belief and will rationalize the conclusion in favor of this belief or will ignore or discredit the data.

So here we are with a world full of brains which do not function alike. Every brain that sees something rationalizes it in a different manner and arrives at a conclusion and that is what I call **perception**.

Knowing this inherent problem with the brain, there are a certain amount of people who take advantage of it. They do this by knowing that they can influence the thoughts and actions of others.

Every gasoline price sign in the U.S. ends in numbers like $3.99.*9,* which is absurd, but it works almost 100% of the time. The brain knows better, but it prefers the $3.99.**9** and ignores the *.9* which puts the gas at essentially $4.00. Someone out there knows this and successfully manipulates the public to get that extra penny and to buy the gas at this location. People will drive by $4.00 per gallon signs all day to get to one that says $3.99.**9**. The human brain is manipulated this way hundreds of times a year on different subjects.

Every human brain in the world is being carried around by someone with a name and it is his brain that is being manipulated. Everything I have described is why we have hundreds of different types of cars, different colors, different foods, wear different clothes, different churches, and so on.

Although our brains have been influenced by something to make these different decisions, our vulnerability is when we have a limited selection and there are people who want to, and can influence the selection. There are various ways to do this and the most affective is misinformation. This usually being that there is nothing good about the other selection and everything is good about this one. The best prey are the brains which are inclined this way anyway, and the brains which are as yet not locked into a belief. Once the brain is locked in to a belief, they are wasting your breath.

Junk mail in your mailbox is relentless and careful examination of it reveals it to be misinformation. You have won a new car and so on. Why does it just keep coming if it doesn't work?

Of course the area of endeavor which is most importance and with the least amount of choices is politics. This being the case, there is a more intense effort by more people to influence you to decide in their favor. Millions are spent on political ads in this effort. The intent being to influence you to either donate money to a particular party or vote for their candidate. Regardless of the party, the option are: stating that you are absolutely correct in voting for our candidate on his merit or you are wrong for not voting for him because the other candidate is guilty of numerous unsavory acts. The brain seems to like negative advertising much more than it does matters based upon their own merit and is easily influenced by it. The negative advertising is such that it is not possible to believe in or be in favor of both sides and the brain goes with the negative ads which it is already bias towards, or if not bias, will fall for the most negative ads in quality or quantity. In respect to politics, most brains have already determined their selection before there is any advertising, as they are bias to a particular philosophy. The millions spent on advertisements have a purpose other than persuading an undecided voter. This barrage of constant negative advertising is also to intimidate anyone from acknowledging that they do not favor that group or candidate. It is the old peer pressure thing. If you have friends or acquaintances who are beyond reasonable discussion of the political issues, then you are condemned to silence. The person who said you should not argue religion or politics said a mouthful. Reason and friendship will go out the window right along with the logic and rational thought.

It is sad that this is the case, but what is merely a democratic election of individuals, has now been converted to hatred and fanaticism. Two groups of people with the same information have arrived at opposite conclusions. This is in no small part to the fact that neither side has any credibility and our government is destined to be run by groups diametrically opposed to each other. And then we wonder why they can't seem to agree on anything.

(50) Native Americans

The first visitors to North America were confronted with the fact that it was already occupied. The Native Americans, called Indians for reasons we all know, greatly outnumbered the new immigrants. These immigrants were aware of other primitive cultures in the world, but none quite like the one they encountered. The American Indians were very tribal in nature and these tribes were distinctly different. Their physical characteristics were different as well as their dress and their entire lifestyle. Although American Indian tribes are all similar in some respects, they are all different in others. The similarities of the European immigrants, although from different countries, were culturally quite similar. Early dealings with the different tribes was quite perplexing to the new immigrants due to the great number of tribes and the differences in attitude towards the early immigrants. If for no other reason than religious beliefs, there was an immediate racial prejudice towards the Indians. I have no reason to believe this is not always the case when a more socially and technologically advanced group of people move to a land mass inhabited by what they considered to be primitive people. It became quite evident to the new American immigrants that they were dealing with many tribes, which by European standards were quite savage and had quite different philosophies in respect to violent confrontations as a way of life. American Indians had been hunter-gatherers for thousands of years and this had become a problem due to their increased populations. The act of hunting and gathering involves large areas of land and with the large populations of tribes and sub tribes, they had been coming in constant contact with other tribes, which usually resulted in a violent confrontation. This was such that for hundreds of years it had become a way of life. By various means, the new immigrants were to a great extent able to bargain with the Indians, usually because the Indians wanted the goods the immigrants were willing to trade to the Indians. For a couple hundred years, the immigrants, colonies or States were able to assimilate Indians into the land now possessed by the immigrants. This was in large part due to the decreasing population of Indians due to European diseases. Lewis and Clark journals explain in great detail the nature of the American Indians they encountered on their journey. As American immigrants continued to spread west, it was at the expense of the American Indians. By what is now called aboriginal rights; the Indians should have owned all of the land that their ancestors had utilized for thousands of years. This was given little consideration when European nations claimed vast portions of North America while the Indians were still occupying it. As one could expect, the ever-increasing numbers of now called *settlers*, was becoming intolerable. Indians performed atrocities against these settlers and they responded in the same manner. As we all know, in the long run the settlers overwhelmed the Indians and with the use of treaties as the final solution, we are where we are at today in respect to American Indians, and a lot of racial prejudice still exists. Racial prejudice does not exist because of the atrocities incurred by whites and the Indians, but is now an attitude due to the cultural differences and the reservation problems. Any prejudice against American Indians is held by the same people who are prejudice of other races or cultures, so the Indians are not specifically picked out for racial prejudice.

There are some of the more well-read and intelligent people who have a great respect for the past Indian cultures and the intellect of the Indian leaders.   There is no admiration for the atrocities the settlers or the U.S. Government committed, as there is none for the atrocities committed by the Indians.

I am of the opinion that there are many misperceptions of the lifestyle and actions of early American Indians and these misperceptions have been promoted for the most part by the Indian nations themselves and some environmentalists.

It has been perceived that the American Indians were great environmentalists. I have never read any account or historic event that bears this out, in fact quite the contrary. My knowledge of Indian tribal societies life style and culture makes this quite understandable and I doubt if they had any concept of environmental practices. All other early societies around the world have developed in the same manner. You can liken it to having an extended camp in the outdoors. You have a fire, which you have to maintain, and the first dead wood you burn is that nearest to the fire. As time passes you travel further to find dead wood until you reach a point that it is not acceptable to travel and carry wood that far, hence you move your camp to another area. This has been done by all peoples with the Earth's resources, including the food supply for hunter-gatherers. This is most likely the reason for the spread of humans on the continents and even to other continents due to running out of resources. At some point in human history it was discovered that the cultivation of crops and the domesticating of animals eliminated this need for constant movement. This did not take place overnight but was a slow transition. After acquiring large herds of domestic animals, the people created the same problem they had originally, whereby the food consumption of the animals required the constant movement. Most of the American Indians prior to the spread of the new immigrants throughout North America were not confronted with this situation in respect to running out of resources. They did move frequently, but it was a planned move developed through the centuries. It was true that most of the non-renewable consumable wildlife was depleted in areas of their camps or villages, but they were not dependent on this source. Although there were countless edible plants as a secondary and supplemental food source, which was an annual renewable source, the primary source of food was available to them in absolutely unbelievable quantities. The food sources were the migratory American bison and the fish spawning runs. The Indians would place themselves in the path of these renewable resources and harvest whatever they desired to consume and preserve until the following year.

Did the Indians harvest more than was necessary? Certainly. They would drive hundreds of bison off cliffs and process what they could until the remaining would spoil. It was the same with salmon as to over harvest. Who in their right mind would under harvest? Was there any consideration give to conservation? No. It was an unheard of concept. If a tribe killed 100 bison or 10,000 bison, it had no effect on the 60,000,000 available to them. Indians saw the banks littered with millions of dead spawned out salmon and I am sure it never crossed any Indian's mind that they could diminish future supplies, because they could not. Indians burned thousands of acres of forest for hunting and plant food gathering purposes. Did they have a problem with this and the preservation of effected species? No. The American Indian for thousands of years had a hard life, but depleting natural resources was not a problem. Further evidence of what today we would consider unacceptable was the trading of infant beaver pelts, wild bird eggs etc. Thousands of years of culture and lifestyle had left the American Indians with no perception of conservation.

The advancing settler population spread across North America and did so with a hunter gatherer mentality. They shot and ate everything that moved with hunting parties always in the field. Those families or groups, who stopped and settled instead of going further west, pretty well consumed all of the wildlife in the area. Even after fields were cultivated, the hunting of wildlife was an important source of food. This was not always looked on favorably by the Indian population and some of these settlers paid the ultimate price for it. In the 1800's, the settlers and native populations became intolerant of each other. The obvious villain being the settlers as the Indians had been living a viable existence there for thousands of years. We are aware of the outcome of the conflict with the confinement of the Indians and we had also devastated the wildlife resources of North America. If it were not for some prominent individuals and government legislation, we would have shot wildlife out of existence. So much for the immigrant's conservation values as well as the Indian's.

How in the hell do you shoot 60,000,000 buffalo and tens of thousands of Indians and walk around with this false pride of how the west was won? It is not likely that what happened to Custer evened the score, but strangely enough it does in the minds of the general public.

The Indians saw the same events as the settlers and have a completely different perception of the problem in the 1800's.

I did not address the southwest Indians who early on developed crop cultivation, as they were culturally different than the others and for the most part occupied land the new settlers did not want.

(51) American industry

The history of American industry that we are so proud of and developed in this country, can be described as a matter of ignorance by today's public as well as a misperception. The industry in this country grew to the giant it was in the late nineteenth and early twentieth century due to the abuse and poverty of the American worker. Giant industrial complexes, which included steel, oil, railroads, shipping, mining, cotton and goods manufacturing and the millionaires it produced, owe this to the mistreatment of workers.

During this era, the workforce was predominantly new immigrants who had nothing when they hit our shore and continued to have nothing while working the remainder of their life. To put things in the correct perspective, we must remember this, because it is our obligation to remember the actual history.

We must not forget slavery which made it possible for there to be the first wealthy people in this country. This wealth enhanced all new industry and the cotton cloth mills. The fabric and clothing industry was a huge sweatshop industry where females and children worked over twelve hours a day in the stifling heat breathing cotton fibers all day and night. Their meager wages when added to other family member's wages, made it possible to barely exist.

Child labor in this country was a significant percentage of the work force. They worked their childhood away for next to no income and in the most unimaginable conditions. There are many existing photos of children working in the garment, and coal industry. It is not a pretty sight.

Immigrants were hired right off the dock for these dangerous low-paying jobs and they took these jobs out of desperation to feed their families.

Let's not forget the company store. This is where you usually owed more money than your paycheck and the paymaster was sure the store was paid before the worker was. Of course the company store was the only store in town and the prices were higher than they should be. People worked for years and never got out of debt to the company store. Leaving was not an option as violence and retribution of family members was the result of that.

How many coal miners are buried in those old mines and how many children died from black lung we will never know. We do know the life expectancy was way down in years and one could argue a case for negligent homicide. All of the cowboys at $10.00 to $30.00 per month for daylight to dark and more, for six or more months at a time and one can only imagine the conditions in the steel and the oil industry.

This is where the old money originated. Millions were made by a few and their lifestyle was extravagant, whereas almost the entire labor force of the U.S. were little more than slaves. The settlers and farmers were probably the lucky ones as they usually had food to eat for their daylight to dark work, but little else.

This is what happened, and my perception of this is nothing for us to be proud of. I am not knocking the U.S. alone, because the rest of the world was in the same situation. Do not entertain the idea that the champions of industry had any conscience towards the working class. Henry Ford broke from tradition, but on his own terms and in his own best interest. And let's not forget "The Grapes of Wrath and Tobacco Road"

This was the way it was all of the way up into the middle twentieth century and until after the depression. The turning point for our society seemed to be during the Roosevelt administration and the influence of the Second World War. During the war years, labor was scarce. The government was paying the bill on contract work, with some oversight, and the industrial magnates seemed to develop somewhat of a longtime in coming, pride in their workers. This quickly diminished with the advent of labor unions.

Most of the history of the misery of workers during these periods can be laid right at the feet of the industrial magnates and the lack of government legislation in respect to labor. Quite obviously, there were not many illiterate poor workers in the Congress at the time. Business was good with no social benefits, no safety laws, no income tax and untold business opportunities. Oh what a life it must have been for the rich. Well, the Titanic leveled the playing field somewhat. The top deck sank just as fast as the bottom deck.

(52) Heroes

There are heroes and then there are heroes. The German people perceived Adolph Hitler as a hero. It is easy to see why the German people rallied around Hitler as he was telling them what they wanted to hear and was very adamant about it. All things considered, what he was spouting was realistic, and he was conceivably the world's best patriot and was not a far cry from what you hear from some country's leaders today. The fact that he was just misleading a bunch of people who thought they were right, is no less than what is happening today.

Other heroes such as Audie Murphy, did not talk themselves into that status. They performed the tasks before they were declared heroes. You can say the same for the heroes on flight 93 on 9/11.

Of course wars are where most heroes are made due to the violent circumstances. In reality most of us are heroes just sitting around for a situation to arise whereby we take action as necessary. There are situations where almost all of us would react in such a manner that we would be declared heroes. It may have to be a different situation for each of us, but we are all potential heroes.

Then there are sports heroes, but I will have to tone this down to what I will call hero worship. Hero worship is for the player that makes the winning catch or the winning kick. But hero worship is almost always in the eyes of the beholder. A fan of the other team thinks the player is a jerk.

(53) Celebrities

Hero-worship and what makes celebrities is a close call.

My perception of a celebrity is someone who has aroused the public due to their wealth, abilities or their notoriety. I do not have what it takes to have the passion and total admiration for other people, which would elevate them to that status. I respect that if there is a person who is talented and everyone thinks is talented, they are a celebrity,

115

but I can not understand yelling and screaming, saving pictures and reading persistently about the person. Celebrities are made by people who do just this. An excellent singer, even though they might have had voice training, was born with the inherent ability and that is no great accomplishment. If he was not born with it he would be driving a taxi or something. Most celebrities turn out to be jerks. Was he a jerk before he was a celebrity or because he became a celebrity?

Some celebrities continue for years and some are just a flash in the pan. Some celebrities who are jerks last for years and I don't really understand how an established jerk maintains the status.

Almost everyone wants to be a celebrity. The average American would almost kill to achieve that status and some do. Celebrities live a life almost unimaginable to me. The lack of privacy, everyone saying yes all of the time, lots of money, everyone wants to marry one instantly, and so on. Young girls are goggle eyed over celebrities and go to all lengths to identify with them. I will have to admit that there are a few celebrities who I would like to meet, not for the notoriety of being with them, but because I admire their qualities. Of course most of these are now probably gone as they were older than me and that means there is a good chance they are dead.

(54) Voting

In the U.S. there is a nationwide perception by everyone excluding a few street people and winos, that it is their absolute duty to vote as a citizen of the U.S. My perception of these people of the U.S., excluding the street people and the winos, is that they are not being rational. This means that I perceive the vast population of the U.S. as being irrational. Well, so be it. The rational perception of whether or not you have to vote to be a patriotic American is that you **do not have to vote.** One of the most important rights we have as citizens of the U.S. is that we do not have to vote. The simple argument for this is that if two candidates are; not qualified, not acceptable in your eyes, are incompetent, are a danger to the U.S., you should vote for neither. Also if you know nothing about them or what you have heard of both is confirmed lies, you should not vote. The people who should vote are the people who have knowledge of who is the best candidate for the job. How 49% of the people decide on one candidate and 51% decide on another tells me that there is more going on here than is rational. That being the case, I must be correct in that almost everyone is irrational.

Beyond that, there are and have been countries, where like here, it is perceived as your duty to vote. The difference being is that in some other countries, if you don't vote for the obvious candidate, you get tortured or shot. For myself, the real patriot is a person who refuses to vote for someone who will be detrimental to the United States. Peer pressure to vote for voting's sake benefits no one. It in fact can easily offset the vote of someone who knows which candidate is the best candidate. It is also not rational or acceptable to me that a person should have to declare his party affiliation or that he is an Independent. I perceive this to be personal information to be declared only if you wish. If asked, a person would surely fall into one of the groups, but having to declare this information is an invasion of privacy. I understand that this matter is to facilitate the voting procedure, but from my point of view, everyone should be an independent. The term itself explains my position. It implies that there is no dependency or obligation to any group which you otherwise would be part of. A person belonging to any organized group is highly susceptible to the doctrine and the peer pressure of that group. This has an impact on any communications he has as to the philosophy of the group and tends to polarize the group and the expectations of voters in that group in respect to a common philosophy. There are millions of people on the fringe of this philosophy in thought, and are influenced by others not to educate themselves to options outside this philosophy. This is likened to flock of sheep being tended by a sheep dog.

Evoking ones freedom as a citizen of the U.S. should be a situation where the citizen has certain obligations to this country, but this does not include joining a philosophical group to do so.

The repercussions of polarizing philosophies are no more evident than in Congress. The entire procedure of legislation and even the seating is based upon it.

You could not get (satirically) 100 people to agree on anything outside of Congress, but when in the building, you get overwhelming partisan votes. There are a few who break from tradition, but usually there is a reason beneficial to them and the rest of their party accepts this to a limited degree.

(55) Famine in the U.S.

Not so much now, but in the past, there was a lot of publicity given to the subject of not being able to feed the population of the U.S. This is *old* news, but I have pondered on this thought for years. It was publicized as, not if, but when. Now the subject may be *new* news in that there are food products available, but they are becoming unaffordable, which is much the same situation. Why they are becoming unaffordable is another matter, but they are becoming unaffordable depending on your financial status.

I see a single large onion in the store for $2.00 and I think to myself, "That is ridiculous; I could raise 10,000 of them in my back yard." Aha. I really could raise 10,000 in my back yard and it wouldn't cost me hardly anything. Right now I am raising grass. I water it, fertilize it, work all summer on it, pay $100.00 a month to have it mowed and hauled off. With presumably a little more effort I could just replace the grass with onions. I assume I could get at least 50 cents each for $2.00 onions. And why am I raising five trees that the only product from them is leaves I have to rake and haul off. There must be a market for fruit and nuts.

And then if my five adjacent neighbors partnered up with me, we could buy bulk fertilizer, split the expense of any equipment, share the labor, etc.

Do you know how many people in this country are raising grass and elm trees? I don't, but I would guess 30,000,000 or so.   30,000,000 times 10,000 onions is 300,000,000,000 onions. That's about 1000 onions for every man woman and child in the U.S. and the fruit from 100,000,000 apricot trees. These apricots and onions could be any fruit or nut and the onions could be a vast variety of vegetables. My point being that famine in the U.S. is not an issue; due to this concept. The price of groceries is, and I suspect that in the foreseeable future you will see this concept-taking place. My reason for addressing this matter is that the scarcity of food or affordable food is a frequently discussed issue and I have never heard this concept being discussed. I am not hungry and can afford food at the moment, but when I can't, at least I have a plan.

(56) Discrimination

My perception of discrimination is the act of any individual or group who denies equal rights or opportunities to another individual or group because they are not similar to the denying group. The most common types of discrimination and the ones recognized by all citizens are racial and age discrimination. The U.S. government has tried to limit these types of discrimination by the legislative process although the desire to discriminate is still there. I would like to address the lesser or unknown types of discrimination. These types of discrimination for the most part are legal, as they are considered frivolous. Every person has experienced discrimination in one form or another and all are guilty of it, assuming there is something wrong with all discrimination.

Physically every person is different due to genetic traits as well as environmental effects. Some people are short, some are tall, some are fat, some are skinny, some have different shades of skin color, hair color, and a multitude of different physical characteristic. You have certainly heard many times the importance of first impressions. This is true to the point that most love relationships and love bonds are based upon first impressions. Beyond this positive effect or negative effect, depending on your experience, most discrimination has negative effects upon society. There are maybe a few who cannot relate to the psychological effect of discrimination. If you have ever been picked dead last to be on a team, you know exactly what I am referring to. During your entire life, there will or have been people selected before you due to your appearance. I mention this because there are people who are not aware of just how discriminatory they are. It works this way. If you are an 18-year-old extremely attractive female with a knockout body, not too short and not taller than males, with an IQ not too high or too low, you are at the high end of the spectrum. The opposite of this female is at the low end. If a selection is to be made on appearance alone, all of the females below her will be discriminated against. This discrimination is based upon first appearance and usually outweighs other considerations. Of course you can see that this is from a male point of view. There are multitudes of reasons the high ender may not be selected, but then number two on the high end has the next best opportunity. Some of the reasons for going down lower in the spectrum are, wives of the selector, intellectual, artistic, hard-working, etc, etc. But still, all of the people above you on the spectrum have the advantage. Most of the people on the low end of the spectrum are aware of this situation although it is rarely discussed out of consideration for these people's feelings. The people on the high end rarely discuss it because they do not want to admit to their unfair advantage. The cosmetic industry thrives on this scenario.

Males are somewhat different as to their position on the spectrum because they can displace the first impression of appearance with similarity in interests with the interviewer or their superior intellect and skills.

As appearance is a genetic trait and is inherited, if you are near the bottom of the spectrum, your ancestors probably were also. Discrimination for generations will inevitably put you in the lower classes of society whether socially, psychologically or financially. This may be obvious to an observant person. Like every other social situation, there are people who are able to break out of these lower classes to the great benefit of their decedents. Wealth has a great deal to do with your position on the spectrum and can also have an effect upon the genetic situation due to marrying up in physical attributes. Females are acutely aware of their appearance and how it affects their lives. They fight the appearance battle on a daily basis.

As for myself, I am short and I have many times experienced being picked last for a team. Hell, there were even big girls selected before I was. The fact that I could run faster and throw further was totally unacknowledged by my teammates.

With this all in my head, I often hear discriminatory or prejudicial comments about the people on the low end of the spectrum such as; they are low class, the criminal element, dumb, etc, etc. I look at them and think 95% of them never had a chance right out of the chute (that being a Freudian slip) from the day they were born. And the longer these people are at the bottom, the less they care and the more they realize they do not have a chance to become part of the society living the good life. This leads to high crime rate, high unemployment, receiving every conceivable social benefit and a dislike for the government and the wealthy. I reiterate here that the wealthy had better keep an eye on this situation as these people develop a have nothing to lose attitude, and a year in prison is like them going to college.

(57) Mental visual images

Speaking only for myself, I have my perception of the visual mental abilities of my brain and I assume that everyone else experiences the same phenomenon.

Fundamentally, when someone asks me what 211 plus 212 adds up to, I see a mental flashcard with a 211 over a 212 and a line beneath them. I just add them and put numbers below the line and I see that number which is 423. The spelling of words is somewhat the same process in that at least I get a visual image of the word and read it.

I have no reason to believe other than everyone's mind works in this manner to some degree. Although, I have known people who had extreme difficulty with spelling and I wondered about that. As I got past forty, I noticed that I would call up an image of a word and it would not appear or I could not make it out. My ability to do math using mental vision became more difficult because I could not remember the numbers I was working with or the answer digits would disappear. I have addressed mental images before, but I would add that mental images are a snapshot of your perceptions of a topic condensed into a distinct interpretation of your perceptions. They may appear as a series of snapshots but still are immensely condensed into these images. As an example, if I were to say bias news network, an image pops into your head of one, two or three people sitting at a TV station news desk. Depending on your own bias and your snapshot, it may be at MSNBC or FOX news. There are many examples of this topic that you know about, but this pops into your head and must be your condensed perception. The same thing happens regardless of the topic, but as I said earlier you may see a short series of images. What we have here folks is a computer monitor and your brain being the computer. We think in images just as we dream in images. A picture is worth a thousand words and if we thought in text we would never complete a thought.

As another example of mental visual images and perceptions, there is something I think about occasionally. This concerns the calendar. When you say any month to me, I visualize a sphere or doughnut shape made of 12 boxed months. The months run counterclockwise with January starting at the 12:00 position on the left and followed by February starting at the 11:00 position. Say any date to me and I locate it in the month on this visual calendar. As the months pass, I end up on Dec. 31st and the 1st of January is at the beginning of a month with as an example, 2012 over it. I don't know if I have ever seen a calendar depicted this way in real life, other than a Mayan calendar. I think it is how I rationalize time as a continuous thing. Giving it more thought than it deserves, what I am seeing is the end of a never-ending spiral.

My point being, that is my perception of a calendar and I suspect I may be in the minority on this one, but we all had the same experiences and my perception is different. This makes me question if people's perceptions are actually due to the information they have experienced or is to some degree decided by your brain, regardless of what you have seen or experienced.

(58) Are you running your brain or is it running you?

I have reason to believe that in more cases than not, your brain is running you. It is processing the information it receives and regardless of the accuracy or inaccuracy of the data, your brain arrives at a conclusion and a course of action. There is a lot of scientific medical evidence that there are issues that the brain is inherently inclined to make bias conclusions about. These are usually emotional issues or are due to the type A, Type B personality thing. You have no control over your type A personality; it is a function of the brain and is running you. For this reason, my perception is that regardless of what one might instantly think about an issue, they should give it a lot of thought because there is a good chance what they think may not be correct. One should also be aware that the people they are listening to have the same problem as they do and they may be predetermined to have a position not based upon rational, logic. Can you change your brain's conclusion on an issue? Sometimes, if the conclusion is not correct and your brain will accept this and by adding additional new information or conflicting information. But always be aware that the brain is easily tricked and manipulated; even mine and yours.

(59) The Gulf of Mexico oil spill

This is a classic example of an industry regulating itself. For decades the oil companies have been drilling and pumping oil out of the gulf. Royalties were paid to Louisiana in the billions and the port facilities in or near New Orleans have been quite profitable also. The bottom line is that Louisiana is an oil-structured State. When the accident occurred, the magnitude of the spill was reported as considerably less than it actually was. I watched the news channels continually as to the progress or no progress that they were making in shutting down the well. I worked in an oil field for several years and am not totally ignorant of the industry. As the spill increased, the State of Louisiana and the fishermen and resorts were the first to start bitching and complaining about how much money the spill was going to cost them and the damage to the fishing industry. The oil companies did the same thing in Louisiana as they did in

Alaska during the Exxon Valdez spill. They hired or leased every gulf fishing boat that would float. Like in Alaska, the Louisiana fishermen were happy as larks and making more than fishing. The oil company then hired everyone they could find whose job would be lost due to the spill and dressed them in vinyl suites with absorbent pads and garbage bags to pick up the hundreds of thousands of gallons of oil expected to hit shore. Watching this was almost humorous, if it hadn't been so pathetic. The bottom line here is that they were paying people they would have to pay anyway, and that stopped the whimpering and the additional negative press. This is a tried and proven system. The State of Louisiana, due to the presence of the press did its share of whining about the spill and the oil company's lack of preparedness in the event of a spill. Now wouldn't you think a state receiving billions of dollars from the oil rigs and sitting in proximity to over 1000 wells, capped or producing, would have an adequate spill response of their own to deploy.

Oh well, the spilled oil has disappeared and I haven't heard a word out of Louisiana as their oil workers are all back to work and they are still using the same defective model blowout preventers they were using that caused the spill. Oh yeah, I understand we were paying subsidies to the oil company while the spill was in process, while the company was using a tax loophole to limit taxes paid to the U.S. You might want to verify this.

(60) Hypocrisy in America

We are a nation of hypocrites in a world full of hypocrites. My perception of hypocrisy is when an individual or group is critical of another individual or group due to their beliefs or actions, while partaking in beliefs or actions which are similar.

It should be obvious to anyone that every person has different character and you can bet that there is someone who is critical of it, or for the most part everyone else's because they are not are not identical to them in body and thought. This in fact is self-righteousness and everyone has it except some individuals who are taking medication because they don't have it. Not having this self-righteousness would be likened to losing your identity.

There are so many examples of hypocrisy in this country that I can only point out a few. One example is religious groups in this country. My perception of the difference between groups such as Jews, Christians, Muslims and so on, is that there is little difference. They all have one absolute identical belief. That being in a Supreme Being or entity. They believe that this Supreme Being or entity is the highest power and their lives and actions are in compliance with the wishes of that Supreme Being or entity. For one group to be critical of another for pursuing their beliefs is hypocritical because they are all doing the same thing.

A person or group who is critical of a person on social welfare and who also enriches himself in anyway by acquiring any government funds or in many cases some of the money paid to the welfare participant is also a hypocrite. A million-dollar grant or subsidy is little different than a welfare check. This is highly arguable because people who receive funds from the government can claim, "Yes, but we need it," or "Yes, but we work for it." There are many people who receive $5000.00 a month government checks for doing little or nothing, while the welfare participant receives $1000.00 a month for doing nothing. It is little different, but yes it is different. I expect the welfare participant has a more stressful time of it managing $1000.00 a month than the other person does managing $5000.00. The private sector has hundreds of programs whereby it receives federal funds or grants or subsidies for reasons beyond what is the most cost-effective means. These in effect are social and economic programs sponsored by the federal government. There are thousands of people on welfare because they are satisfied with $1000.00 of government money every month and don't have to do anything. There are also people satisfied with $10,000.00 every month of government money and they don't have to do anything either.

Now for those hard working people, who are paid by the government, this matter does not include you and you know who you are. Well, I guess it does, or the critical term "Government Worker" wouldn't be used by hypocrites that think that their walking a mile is much harder than you walking a mile.

Because we are all hypocrites by nature, the worst kind of hypocrite is the self-righteous one who doesn't know he is a hypocrite. My God, I am a hypocrite and I can't help it. But I know I am a hypocrite, and knowing that fact means that I have to adjust my perception of things and adjust my actions towards everyone else in the world.

You know people who seem to bitch about everything and everybody, as well as you, when you are not around. These are the people who lack the humility they would have adopted if they knew they were hypocrites.

These are rough examples of hypocrisy, but I think society would run a lot smoother if at least everyone recognized that they are hypocrites to some degree.

(61) Stalkers (a hypocritical term)

This is a term that can be applied to everyone above the age of puberty, as we have all practiced it. In fact it is normal behavior for both sexes and is a function of the brain's behavior in order to satisfy its needs for sexual satisfaction or the acquiring of a mate. Without this stalking behavior, acquiring a desired wife or husband would be impossible. Boy meets girl, boy chases girl or vice versus. When one or the other decides that this is the person for them, the stalking begins. The watching from your car, the accidental meetings, the accidental phone calls, making of mutual friends and all of the other crazy humiliating things a person does to acquire this mate, requires a lot of stalking. Online love connection networks can do a lot of the stalking for you, but you still have to do a considerable amount yourself to end up in a matrimonial situation.

Now the downside to stalking is that if it is discovered and the other person is a willing participant, it is perceived as being admirable and appreciated behavior. On the other hand if it is discovered and the other person is not a willing participant, it means big trouble. The stalker is identified as a nuisance, all of the way to it being a criminal offense. The sad thing about the normal, average, found the girl of his dreams person is that he does not know when to stop stalking and in almost every case can't stop. This is love and the driving force is immense. Many young people have paid the ultimate price because they can't stop loving and stalking and many have had legal problems and many, many, more have had to relocate to prevent stalking.

My reason for discussing this issue is that the term stalker is perceived by the general public as a reprehensible act when in fact they have all been stalkers at one time or another. I admittedly have been a stalker and like millions of other people, it worked out great for the wife and me. I don't think most people acknowledge their actions for what they were or are, and in the old days they may have referred to it as courting. But in fact, they were doing the same thing that the truly criminal stalker does and he is motivated usually by the same brain functions. In some cases their intent is the same until they find out that a relationship is impossible and act violently or they are just sexual predators driven by their brain, which may have some real issues.

(62) Modern dancing

I can truthfully say that nothing embarrasses me more than to see a grown man out on the dance floor gyrating and making a complete fool of himself. It embarrasses me and I am at the back of the room sitting down. I don't know why it embarrasses me, but I say to myself, "Look at that fool." It may be a modesty thing, I don't know. I was raised and grew up with the notion that you were not supposed to make a fool or a spectacle of yourself. I will usually give the fool the benefit of the doubt and say he is drunk and has no inhibition. That is about my limit for excuses. Well, maybe not. He may be stalking or courting, but then again, I have seen people going through these motions with their wife. Oh well, maybe he doesn't have any choice.

I suspect my perception of this display may ruffle some feathers, but that is how I see it.

In my defense, I think Ginger Rogers and Fred Astaire were marvelous dancers, but then again, they were getting paid for it. I can even appreciate the talent in ballet, but none of this even closely resembles the fool going through motions that wouldn't even be recognizable by a drugged up Aztec dancer.

(63) Water

This is a troubling topic to address because the topic is so comprehensive in nature. With it we may survive, but without it there is no chance in hell. There was a time that water was not as much of a problem as it is today. People went to where there was water and they knew how much water was there and they adapted and developed to that quantity. The issue of water use, the depleting water supply and how we have not planned for reduced supplies makes me tired and I want to just give up on the matter.

Why we have not developed means of moving unwanted water to areas starving for water is beyond me. Houses are floating away in some places while crops are dying from lack of water in others. People will migrate from areas where the water is drying up and areas with water will gladly give them water if they will just stay where they are.

(64) Prohibition

The general perception of the passing and repealing of prohibition is that the passing of the legislation was a mistake and the repealing of the legislation was to rectify that mistake. The passing of the legislation was instigated by a bunch of do-gooders or religious people who were predominantly women.

Some of this may be true, but it is a shame that the American public is not aware of the realty of the situation when the legislation was passed and when it was repealed. We may have heard of the old lady smashing up bars with a hatchet and we all have surely heard of Al Capone, both of which were major players in this matter.

The reality of the situation prior to passing prohibition into law was that the use and abuse of alcohol (predominantly by men) in the U.S. can be compared to a pandemic. The consumption of alcohol by males in the U.S. was not only the most popular social function; it was a lifestyle that resulted in widespread alcoholism. We were a nation of drunks and all of the bad aspects of drunken behavior were taking place. This usually resulted in the mistreatment of family members and the depletion of financial resources necessary to support a family. The wives and children of these alcoholics were not protected by society or the government and for the most part their life was Hell. Not to say that there are not some friendly drunks.

This alcoholic scourge on society, usually the lower classes and poorest, did not happen overnight. The first colonists arriving in America were heavy drinkers (excluding some religious groups) and had a vast knowledge of how to produce alcohol. Rum, cider and whisky were the most common alcoholic beverages and were consumed on a daily basis. Our earliest colonists drank alcoholic beverages as today we drink water, soft drinks, etc. In respect to the founders of this country, they may have had some social and political rules as to working under the influence of alcohol, but I suspect they were not all that effective. Not to say that our forefathers were all intoxicated when the framework for this country was set up or even that they could not do a good job when tipsy. I do suspect however that it may have played a part in the disagreements and dislike among the members.

The brightest of our ancestors were well aware of the downside of alcohol consumption to excess and alcoholism. Therefore they had the best chance of avoiding it. There was no great aversion to drinking alcohol, as there was none to smoking in the 1940,s and it was normal social behavior. The highest social classes had the wealth and means to pursue other interests whether it was business interests, politics, or other entertainment. Whereas the lower classes had little else in the way of social interaction or enjoyment.

George Washington at one time was the largest producer of consumption alcohol in the country. This in no way detracts from his character, as it was just another business.

By the time prohibition was passed into law, and due to the increased masses of population living in the poorest of conditions, the repercussions of the intoxicated male population upon families and their financial existence was at the point it was not tolerable by most of the female population, as well as our society in general. The end result appeared to be an imminent collapse of the society. Female activists hit the streets with banners and so on to protest the abuse and their children's living conditions. As can be expected, I assume a lot of women took a beating for their efforts, but a lot of women were taking beatings anyway.

Prohibition was passed by Congress. This is what is perceived today as being a mistake and the government trying to legislate morality. Well, we can all be a judge of this perception.

The repeal of prohibition is perceived to be to rectify the mistake of enacting it. The grounds for repealing the prohibition act was that it was decided that you cannot legislate morality, particularly when most of the eligible voters did not agree with the legislation. In reality the prohibition act did relieve a lot of the family issues and society was better off for it on the family level, which was the primary problem.

Congress was correct in that at the time of repeal it was not a popular amendment; although it wasn't popular when it was passed into law either.

When prohibition was amended into the Constitution, it created a whole new social problem, which was more troublesome for Congress than the original problem. Organized crime took over the distribution of alcohol to the U.S. public (I might add that it was too expensive for the lower classes), but there were moon shiners to assist this problem.

Congress was faced with the bloodshed of organized crime, unheard of corruption of public officials and the police, the power of organized crime in confrontation with the Congress and a major factor was that the U.S. Government and economy was losing millions of dollars in the manufacturing industry and potential tax revenue. The government had lost control of the ability to enforce unlawful alcohol consumption and distribution and the situation was getting worse. Therefore, prohibition was repealed.

For a variety of social and economic reasons, the general population of the U.S. did not revert back to the mass alcoholism status it had prior to prohibition, but many families have had to deal with the problem of alcoholism since then.

Now, the more dominant social issue in respect to addiction and the social implications is due to illegal drugs. Did we make another one of these (mistakes) declaring the use and sale of drugs a criminal offense? Are we again trying to legislate morality? This is a good question for the people who have the perception of prohibition being a mistake that was rectified.

(65) Tires and the environment

Something I think about frequently is tires and the environment. Not that tires have a negative impact on the environment, I just think of the numbers involved. I am figuring this out off the cuff as I write, so the numbers are a guess on my part, but reasonable enough to satisfy me. Today there are probably around 100,000,000 cars in the U.S. For the sake of convenience let's say that car owners buy a set of tires every three years. The reason they buy a set of tires every three years is that the tread wears off of them. How exactly it wears off, most of us do not know, it just leaves. As you don't see chunks of rubber lying around, I think we can conclude that it comes off as extremely fine particles and becomes airborne for some period of time. The airborne time must be considerable because you do not see any evidence of it next to the highway. Well, just how much of it is there and where does it go? Some quick estimates and calculations and I come up with; each vehicle loses about 8 pounds total off its tires each year. If that is even reasonably close, we are putting about 800,000,000 pounds of tire particles into the air every year. Over a 20-year period and adjusting for fewer cars, this comes to about

13,000,000,000 pounds of tire material. Well, where is it? More fun with math and estimated figures reveal that there should be 2100 pounds on every square mile in the U.S. Let's say we go back another 20 years with fewer cars and round it off at 3000 pounds per square mile. One would think that it would settle to earth within hundreds of yards of a highway which eliminates 80% of the U.S. at a minimum and that 3000 pounds per square mile should really be around 13,000 pounds per square mile along the highway and conceivably within a quarter mile of it. I am leaving this to someone else to figure out what happened to it. I just hope it makes good fertilizer and is not bad for our lungs.

(66) Phobias

Phobias are very interesting and a classic example of the perception of things by different people. Some people are afraid of heights while others are free climbers. Some people are petrified by snakes and others sleep with them. The list of phobias is endless and each phobia always by a small minority of people. Some phobias make complete sense, whereas some make no sense at all. Being in an airplane at 35,000 feet and being scared to death (that's me) makes perfect sense, at least to me. Being afraid and having an anxiety attack by looking at a picture of a spider in a book does not. In one instance you **are** in danger as the other you are not. There may be psychologists who can explain in detail what causes phobias, but I doubt it. Having a near drowning experience could well develop a phobia of water, which would be a learned trait. Other bad experiences could well develop other phobias, but it appears to me that it is one part of the brain in conflict with another part. One part knows it is a picture of a spider and is no threat and another part responds to the picture as an imminent threat. My perception of this issue is that the brain has an inherent stimulated response to what it considers is a threat. These are genetic psychological traits.

An example of this is the response of most animals to the first snake they ever encounter. Although the snake is so small it should not be a threat; something in the brain says jump. A horse is by nature what has been defined as being *spooky* and may bolt from a butterfly 10,000 times smaller than the horse.

Phobias for no apparent reason could well be a brains genetic response to a particular thing. As to why all humans don't have identical unexplained responses is a good question. It may be just that all brains are not created equal. There are brains afraid of everything and brains afraid of nothing. The people with unexplainable phobias may have brains that are misidentifying the object or threat. A more plausible origin of phobias is subconscious thought, being dreams.

(67) Dreams

The most important thing I am sure of about dreams, is that nobody wants to hear about your dreams and just cringe when someone talks about their dreams.

Other than that, I have a theory base upon absolutely no scientific evidence I have come in contact with. Dreams are one example of subconscious thought. My perception of subconscious thought is when the brain is performing a certain way when the individual is not conscious of his surroundings. My theory is that the brain plays out multitudes of mental visual scenarios when a person is not conscious. This may be dreams, drug induced unconscious thought and certain comas. When this occurs, the brain is not hitting on all eight cylinders and information is created while other portions of the brain do not react to it or are contributing to it. In most cases the subconscious information is stored in a very inefficient manner, but some of it can be recalled by the conscious brain. This stored unconscious memory seems to fade in a short time. There seems to be no limit to the brain's imagination when it comes to the content of subconscious dream scenarios.

In some cases the dreams or subconscious visions are so distinct and traumatic that a person is wakened by them, and these dreams and others may be stored in long term conscious memory. Some dreams are so emotional and sensitive to the brain that the conscious brain can develop phobias, learn to hate, fall in love, become deeply religious and other afflictions. In a lot of cases the conscious brain may remember things which actually did not happen to them during their life, but are subconscious dreams remembered as actually happening.

Dreams and subconscious visions have been accepted as having some paranormal power for thousands of years. It could be a sign or message from God or the Gods and in many cases humans will wait for these subconscious visions and act on them. If it is not fast enough, the most popular method of receiving subconscious thoughts is by inducing people with drugs to a subconscious or hallucinatory level.

Subconscious thought may play a bigger part in ones life than they think. For myself, understanding dreams and all of the scientific data in respect to them, I have little knowledge, but I am a master at having dreams. Not a night passes I do not dream, and they seem continuous. If I fall asleep in the chair watching TV, I immediately go into a dream state. Some people rarely dream and the dreams are very vague. This is true to some degree myself, but a lot of my dreams I actually read documents, tie fishhooks on lines and so on. I have heard people ask if we dream in color. Trust me, we do, or at least I do.

Dreams can ruin your entire next day by bring up emotionally suppressed subject matter.

Well, I am bored with dreams.

(68) Taste

"Have you tried the new restaurant?"

"No, how was the food?"

"The best food I have ever eaten."

"What did you have?"

"I had the poached mussels in sour cream and shrimp sauce and cauliflower sautéed with eel grass. The wife had the pig brains Flambe covered with a thickened red beet sauce and blanched kelp. She loved it and mine was delicious.

I don't see any point in addressing a topic that everyone knows about, but how can one person be right and most of the world wrong? I guess that is a matter of taste.

(69) Everyone should know

There are things that everyone should know, but of course these things are relative to the society they live with and their location. An Ethiopian really does not need to know how to make snow ice cream, as an example. They will never do it and will never be asked how to do it or even discuss it. There are certainly things that Ethiopians should know because of their society and location, but this is one of many that they don't.

Being a resident of the United States and having the ability to travel internationally, there are things which U.S. citizens should know in order to function in our society. Granted that you can get by without knowing these things, but you run into them frequently as you function within the society. Ninety percent of the discussions whether in person or telecommunications is attributed to telling someone something they do not know. Of course most of this relates to Dancing With The Stars, or what happened on Oprah. These, although they sound trivial will probably be discussed in the future and knowing this information, you can jump right into a discussion and hold your own.

This book contains information that I think every American who is going to be involved in the real world should know. Again this is relative to the individuals and things you will be dealing with the rest of your life. A convicted murderer in prison for life surely needs to know less than an individual working for the State Department, but having a little knowledge of the law would not hurt him.

There are social, intellectual and economic factors that demand a little knowledge. The United States like all other countries is not a classless society. We have poor people, not very intelligent people, rich people, uneducated people, beautiful people, ugly people, athletic people and on and on. Each of these classes of people tend to migrate toward each other as a matter of similar interests and comfortability.

A very short, ugly, poor, unintelligent person will seek out companions of approximately the same level as a matter of psychological self-preservation. Usually there is someone shorter, uglier, and dumber than they are and this makes their social life acceptable. What you need to know at this level is pretty well just how to survive the situation and the price of gold futures or where Darfur is, will probably never come up.

As it seems everyone needs to know different things due to their situation in life, I am going to address only the middle class, average intelligent American with an average amount of ambition. I will address what I perceive this as the knowledge the person should acquire from their sophomore year in high school until they die, whether they are male or female.

This knowledge can best be explained in categories, which makes it immensely easier for the author. There are categories of which some readers have absolutely no interest, but that does not mean that they should not know a little about them.

But first I would like to get the kid out of high school. In order to do this; there are things they should know before they get out into the real world. This is when they should make a great effort to acquire *what they should know* to add to what they already know. By the time the average student is a junior in high school and until they graduate, about half of them, and usually the smart half, have a pretty good idea as to their interests, talents and mental capabilities. These are the people that have a jump at the starting line and the other half are for the most part never going to catch up. So what the dumb half should know is that unless they follow the lead of the smart half, they are going to have a hard time of it after high school. Of course some in the dumb half aren't dumb at all, in fact they may be brilliant, but for other social reasons just pretend to be dumb. These few will make it just fine after high school because they already know what they are going to have to do to play catch-up and are very capable of it.

For those students who are the big and tall athletes in high school and are the school celebrities, they have my sympathy unless they are truly gifted. For most of them, this celebrity status is going to come crashing down around their ears. The good looking young girls who are attracted to this celebrity status and they all are, should know that they should not get overly involved with someone who is going to crash after graduation. Good looking young high school girls should know that they are going to be good looking young ladies when it really counts. Unless of course, if it is Dr. Miller's son who takes a liking to them in high school.

What every graduate should know is that they should have a plan and if they don't by then, they are probably not going to be in that group that has the nice houses on the hills around the city.

Well they are out of high school now and as we are talking about economics, success and relationships to other individuals and that will be our next two topics.

(70) Employment and careers

Being just out of high school and being middle class, there are observations of this group that the author has made. I am not talking about the wealthiest and the most intelligent of the graduating middle class, as they are pretty well set.

For the group who does not have a plan and enrolls in Junior college, if they do not finish junior college and go on to college, the time they spend in junior college could better have been spent in classes that teach hands on labor. Not being a four-year college graduate puts you in a category where employment is at the hands on labor level and the competition is severe and employers have no mercy on the feeble. At this level, the only possible way they are going to advance to any degree is if they know somebody. So it might behoove a young person to be polite to their friends and elders as they grow up. Option two for this group is a Union enrollment, but again, that is nearly impossible unless you know someone in the Union. They have little sympathy also.

Either group, whether the college graduates or non-college graduates, for the most part advance by running a bluff. This is where *"what you should know"* really shines. You do not really have to know about it, but know of it. You have to realize that everyone above you is where they are because they ran the same bluff or have been advanced to the *position of incompetence*.

The author will describe this position. Those people in the workplace who are really trying to get ahead and have ambition, work at a job position until they are absolutely knowledgeable hard working employees, doing an excellent job; the boss sees this and thinks, "That person deserves an advancement in position and a little more money." Everybody is happy until the person advanced realizes that they do not have the knowledge to perform the job they were given, so they have to go into the bluff mode. This is *the position of incompetence*. The boss just lost the best employee he had and doesn't know it until the person taking his place, who is also now in the bluff mode screws up and requires time to come up to speed. Usually the boss is also in the bluff mode all of the time, because he is supposed to know everything all of the employees below him know, and he is counting on the person he has just advanced to the position of incompetence, to help him out. What workers should know is that if they anticipate any advancement, is to prepare for that advancement and study up and ask questions.

In this equation somewhere is why employers like to hire from outside their own company for competent employees.

Any working stiff out there will tell you, it's not easy. The advantage goes to the; Good looking, well mannered, smartest, butt kissing, best bluffing, friend of the family, church member, and those who will work for less, *and not necessarily in that order.* As well, your co-workers are jockeying and competing for advancement and money also. All employees should know this and if they are forty, already do. The secret is to work hard, be friendly and outsmart the rest of them. A certain amount of butt kissing is required, but is acceptable practice in the work place. Now that our high school graduate has fought his way to retirement, whatever that is, we will go back and determine what he must know about money and finances when he graduates from high school.

(71) Money management

The average middle class high school student without college plans used to get a part time job at McDonalds or the like. In the thirties it was to help the family out and in the eighties it was to buy something to help yourself out, such a necessary electronic device, cosmetics or chrome hub caps.

The parents keep telling the students to save their money in hopes they will have all of it when they enter college, or they can afford an apartment if they do not attend college. Either way, the student should know that most parents want their nineteen-year-olds at a comfortable distance, which requires money. But primarily the reason for this separation is that they would like a break before they start raising grandchildren.

Even in their younger years the parents push them to save their pennies. The ones that do adhere to this policy until adulthood are the same ones we contend with that never pick up the check at the restaurant regardless of how much money they have.

In their twenties, our graduates or non-graduates either spend more money than they make or have a little extra. The ones that spend more than they make adapt by joining forces with others that are in the same boat or get married and the spouse works. This is usually the time the parents have been trying to avoid, the raising of the grandchild. What the now working couple should know is that the grandparents, after the initial shock, have deeper feelings for the grandchildren than they did for them. I think it just seems that way to the grand parents as they remember what they had to put up with as parents and they are not with the grandchildren one hundred percent of the time.

Well we will leave the typical non-college graduate and his wife and now two kids as they are not going to have a lot of money to manage anyway and no matter how much they spend or what on, the end result is zero or extremely slow accrued assets.

We will go on to the college graduates and their financial issues. These are invariably the people who bought into the save your pennies thing and as well have been trying to survive on a bare minimum of money for at least four years of college, which compounds their financial philosophy. These graduates are dumped out on the open market at the same time as 500,000 other graduates. The top ten percent are immediately picked up by companies at an entry-level pay scale. Some have anticipated this day and have made arrangements and take employment in positions such as schoolteachers, where there is a normal attrition rate of retirees. What the rest of them should know is that employers have slowly worked the system so that a lot of students have already been working at the company as interns for little or nothing under the assumption that the employer will hire them when they graduate. In most cases they do, but they are probably looking at a six-month trial period with some or no benefits and an entrée level salary even though they have been trained for that position and the entry level pays sounds good as previously they were working for nothing. What all of these people should know is that your employer is no friend of employees that are taking money out of their pocket. It is going to be you against the employer for resources for the rest of your life. Either he gets the money or you do, and he didn't get where he is by giving money away.

But do not despair, you are still making more wages that the non-graduate and you have a little excess. Almost without question you will marry a college graduate who is working and will have the additional salary. Something that is a theory mind you, but just look around. Female college graduates will marry equals or marry up. Male graduates will try, but will go for appearance of the young lady every time. That is why females should know that finding a husband quickly in college is their best bet as there is considerable competition for the males with high potential. Male or female graduates now having employment and a spouse that is employed, has excess money at the end of each week. Now the whole private sector is aware of this and they want that money. It seems like everyone in the world has an absolutely essential product that you must have.   Life insurance companies, health insurance companies, credit card companies, banks, cemetery plots, cruise lines, and they are relentless in their pursuit.   Of course the people contacting you are college graduates like yourself and that just happens to be where they found employment.

As college graduates are frugal by training and out of previous necessity. They are a hard sell on small domestic items, but are for some reason an easy sell on big-ticket items they traditionally purchase.   They buy an $800,000 home and still don't pick up the tab at the restaurant. They are compelled to have new cars so as not to look out of place in the company parking lot.   They opt for the 401k plan, stock options, and daycare center payments because the grandparents didn't follow them to Boston. By nature, they know exactly how much money they have and where it is and every penny of it is drawing interest or appreciating in value.   They are or have been surrounded by people or co-workers who have made hundreds of thousands of dollars in stock, real estate, and other lucrative investments.

Remember the poor non-graduate, well do you think he gives a damn if Microsoft went from $38.00 to $15.00 or the real estate market just crashed?

Well these poor college graduates do as they take their knocks, which to them is devastating as they are so money conscious anyway. What they should know, is not to feel so bad about the situation because every dollar that they lost was a dollar made by another college graduate.

As economics is referred to as a theory, there is really no perfect answer as to what to do with their excess cash. What they should always bear in mind is that somebody else wants it and there is little they won't do to get it. For these reasons, people with money have a great deal more trouble trying to keep it, than a poor person does managing theirs. And like all economics, even by the most intellectual, it is described as a theory mainly because they cannot predict future events.

(72) Time travel

I am just throwing this in here because everyone should read a little bit about Time, Relativity, Physics, Astronomy and other sciences. My perception of these areas of knowledge is that like myself, 95% of what you read you will not understand, but the 5% you do understand will stagger the brain and you will know 100% more than most people about these subjects.

Is time travel possible? If you consider being in a different time than someone else, Yes. The faster you travel, the slower time is and the closer you are to a large gravity source, the faster time is. If you and another person were on the space station and the other person headed out to space at a very high rate of speed and you settled down into the heavy gravity of Earth. *Your* synchronized watch would say 4:00 PM and y*our buddy's* out in space would read 3:00 PM. The reality is that you are an hour older than him than when you were both at the space station. You are actually a little older now than the space station. For this reason, clocks on satellites have to be occasionally adjusted to Earth time

Enough of this, as it is of no consequence to us because in order to travel in time of any significance is beyond what a human body could survive. Aliens, I don't know about.

I am compelled to throw in another quote by Albert Einstein in respect to time. He said, "The only reason for time is so everything doesn't happen at once." Am I the only one who thinks this is as hilarious as I do?

(73) Albert Einstein

While mentioning Albert Einstein, here is a classic example of misperception. The perception of Albert Einstein by the general public is far from the character who was extremely witty and had a terrific sense of humor. I would recommend that everyone go on line and read his famous quotes, which are the reality of physics and his humorous thoughts about his involvement in the field.

(74) Friendship and friends

There are all types of friends. The majority of a person's friends are acquaintances who they have met at their place of employment or at school or church. These are people who they communicate with when they happen to meet each other in public and occasionally in a social setting such as at work, school, dropping by the house and at social functions. These are people with whom they get along well with on a friendly basis. They usually don't agree on all matters, but avoid any altercations with them.

Then there are *true friends*. These are usually people who you have known for many years and frequently communicate with. These are the people you are always glad to see and spend time with if possible. If they move a great distance from you, you keep in frequent contact.

My perception of a *true friend* is a friend with which you can discuss personal problems in confidence. There is a mutual trust among true friends in that each will act in the best interest of the other. A true friend will go to almost any lengths at the request of the other or if there is a personal problem. There are limits to what even a true friend will do for another, but a true friend does not approach this limit. True friends do not always agree on all matters, but each accepts the others position out of respect and these conflicting matters may rise to discussion, but do not go beyond that.

True friends are rare and a person will only have a few during their lifetime. There are friends who would like to be considered true friends, but it takes years to develop a true friendship. The backbone of a true friendship is trust and respect. Trust that you can reveal your most personal information and trust such that they can have access to anything you own with 100% certainty that there will never be a problem.

True friendship transcends any differences between them as these differences are respected by the other.

(75) Torture

My perception of torture is the physical mistreatment of another individual beyond the point of reasonable discomfort as a means of punishment or interrogation. Beyond the point of reasonable discomfort is a gray area and like all gray areas will be abused in a heartbeat with an explanation of what everyone else perceives as reasonable discomfort. We all know what we could tolerate in respect to abuse before we would consider it torture. That is what reasonable discomfort is.

I will say right off the bat that *water boarding* is unquestionably torture. One who denies this should be more than willing to submit to it to numerous times to prove it. Many have been asked to, and none have accepted. Water boarding is simply no more or no less than repeatedly drowning a person, with his brain absolutely convinced he is drowning.   If it is not torture, we owe a couple Japanese families a letter of apology for hanging several Japanese soldiers for performing water boarding on American prisoners.

We did not invent water boarding, as it was a form of torture long before we used the technique. My perception of whether or not any form of torture is acceptable is that the answer has to be, Yes.   There are circumstances where torture would be acceptable, but would have to be approved by the highest command. The highest in command must also be prepared to accept the responsibility. No reasonable person in the world, which includes the enemy, would question the practice of torturing a person if he knew where there was an atomic weapon in a large city which was to be detonated. I would have no problem with pouring the water.

We would have to be near certain of the existence of a bomb and not just randomly torturing people to determine if there is a bomb somewhere or may be in the future. If this were to ever take place, the torturer and the person tortured should cease to exist; unlike being on the 6:00 news and arguing that it is not torture and is legal. My God, that is stupid. The reason it is stupid is that it puts our soldiers or citizens in harms way. As well, prior to us admitting to what everybody really knows is torture, there was only one internationally acceptable reason for us to invade a country on a small scale and that was to rescue a U.S. citizen who was being tortured. We just gave the enemy a license to water board U.S. civilians and soldiers all over the world.

(76) Corporations and the stock market

I have no perception of how these function in reality. I have an idea of how they are supposed to function, but this does not seem to conform to reality. I have more questions about these than answers. I am walking around with the perception of these as follows; A Corporation is a company or group of companies who initially did not have the funds to establish their business venture. The public was told that they could buy a share of the corporation and they would use this money to get the venture operational. For their purchased share they would receive a share of the annual profit proportional to their investment in the corporation. The purchased share would also maintain a value proportional to the value of the assets of the corporation. This could also be a private company who needed additional money for expanding the business. This all makes sense to me to this point. Where I lose it is when corporations give their officers stock options at the expense of the outside shareholder. Then there is the Board of Directors who designate their own wages and bonuses at the expense of the outside shareholder. When the corporation has very good profits, they hold back a large portion of it or spend it on their structures and equipment or they purchase their own stock back from investors. The outside stockholder is at the mercy of the corporation in respect to dividends, which will always be minimal.

Why would a person buy stock in a large corporation and continue to enrich only a few, and the dividends are paying less than treasury notes are paying? Oh, I know, the dividends are not a factor; the money is going to be made when the value of the stock increases. It appears to me that there are two kinds of people who buy stock. Those who know what is going to happen and those who hope it will happen. Those who are hoping are like a leaf blowing in the wind. Whichever way it blows, they are in for the ride.

Insider trading. Now here is a joke. You have hundreds of people aware of what the corporation is going to do. These are all very money-orientated people and every one of them is supposed to keep secret any information which will affect the price of the corporation stock. Give me a break. In most instances any insider trading information which results in stock purchases probably screws the outside shareholder again.

Not that there isn't money to be made in the stock market, but it can also easily be lost. If you can predict the future, that is the place to put your money. Wouldn't a rational person think that for minor adjustments the stock, it would never raise their purchase price and the increase in value of the assets of the corporation would be paid in dividends? You could sell it back to the corporation at what you paid for it if you wanted, or less if the value of the corporation decreased in value. It would be a little more complicated than this, but not much more.

But then what about the stock brokers and the stock market who is taking a slice out of shareholders money and stock purchases? Too complicated for me, but it all smells a little fishy.

(77) Are flowers pretty?

Well of course flowers are pretty, or are they really? Well, all people believe that the many various colored flowers are pretty and even at great distances, fields of flowers are pretty.

I question whether the flowers themselves are pretty, or is it just their color that is pretty? A black and white picture of a flower highly suggests that it is the color that is pretty and not the flower structure itself. In fact, when in ash gray in a black and white photo, some flowers are downright ugly. One might appreciate the flower structure for other reasons, but it would not be described as pretty. This being an example of what I think when someone says, "These flowers are beautiful, and just look at those yellow ones over there."

(78) Political parties

This seems an appropriate time to address political parties. My perception of the concept of political parties as we have them today, is that in a Democratic/Constitutional Republic, they have too much influence over citizens voting options. If you belong to a political party (you **belong** to a political party.) Political parties tend to polarize the population and incite fear, distrust, hinder individual free thought and actions and their votes. To varying degrees, the political parties do not like organized labor unions. Ironically they are almost identical in concept. They both consist of a group of people who have organized themselves to arrive at a favorable outcome for its members when confronting their adversaries. Almost everything about the structure is the same including the lack of remorse for their adversaries. The dues are paid somewhat differently, but they are paid.

Having said this, political parties have been the backdrop for some of the most insidious corruption to be found in this country. There are countless thousands of pages of legislation committed to preventing the corruption of the candidates and the Congress itself, due to political parties and their financial backers. A political party is the most effective way to acquire and manage financial resources for philosophical agendas. Political parties are giant propaganda machines and if it were not for them, we would not know who to vote for. They acquire the power of a block of votes, which can be manipulated to a great degree by the leaders of the party. Like it or not, *they* are selecting the leaders of this country, not the citizens. What it amounts to is that you can vote for any one of the selected candidates. I cannot imagine a grassroots movement for candidates like G.W. Bush or Barack Obama. Neither was known nationally and at the time of their election they had such dubious pasts that if not for the powers that be, they would never have been candidates.

The easiest thing in the world to do is to bitch about something, in this case, political parties. Because I have bitched about them, I should offer a better method for selecting candidates and a means of getting them elected to office. Well, as the system of political parties is not going to change anyway and I have no clue how you would change it at this point, I would be satisfied if every voter in the U.S. became aware of how the political party system functions and the control they have over the voters and their influence in determining specific individuals to hold public office.

Individual voters should have the ability to ascertain if there is any corruption or illegal practices in the party. But in reality, I suspect any die-hard Democrat or Republican is of the opinion that the end justifies the means. Which is what happens when you join a group of like-minded people with the same objective in mind.

(79) Short attention span and instant gratification

a. Short attention span. There are people walking around out there that fall on this end of the spectrum of human personalities. These are the people who never run short of ideas and these ideas are forgotten and replaced in short order. They are also the people who are right all of the time. They never gave the idea or their position the necessary time to ascertain that they were bad ideas or that they were wrong and they don't understand why others don't agree with them. You see this idiosyncrasy in people who talk constantly, and behold, the subject changes by the minute.

b. Instant gratification. These are the people who cannot tolerate activities that consume a great deal of time or thought. You will rarely see this trait in artists and most musicians (other than Jazz musicians.) because they could not forego the long process of learning to play an instrument. They are great TV channel changers also and can actually watch two or three different channels at the same time. These are also the people that want a solution to a problem immediately regardless of the repercussions (because they are closely related to short attention span people and don't have time to think about repercussions.) Both of these types seem to have an abnormal amount of problems.

(80) Teenagers

Teenagers are simply underage crazy people. (Just kidding) You have heard the phrase "Know just enough about something to get yourself in trouble." That pretty well sums it up for teenagers. They have a lot of intelligence and no experience. You have also heard the phrase, "You learn by mistakes." Well this is when all of the mistakes are made while learning and it makes perfect sense to me. The advantage of an older person criticizing teenagers is that they are not being hypocritical because they were at one time teenagers themselves. Few will admit to acting any better when they were teenagers, than today's teenagers they are criticizing.

An interesting thing about teenagers forty or fifty years ago and the teenagers today is how they were treated in respect to unlawful activities. Unlawful activities by teenagers were looked on very harshly by the parents and relatives. They were punished by the parents, unless the kids were absolute outlaws.

Whereas the police were extremely lenient. Incidents where teenagers were caught in the act of being intoxicated or even driving drunk usually ended up with the officers taking the teenagers home and informing their parents. Not in every case, but it was extremely common. Many other offenses were treated in the same manner.

Now, the parents are the first to jump to the aid of their teenagers and little is done in the way of any serious punishment by the parents. On the other hand, now the police officers cannot get them in jail or in front of a judge fast enough. It has been my experience that if you can get kids through those difficult years, they seem to smooth out and pursue goals other than just running crazy. But now, many of them have criminal offenses on their records, which makes that difficult. Not that all teenagers are irresponsible. In fact percentage wise, there are more responsible teenagers now than there were when I was one.

My perception of the teenager problem is that I definitely do not have a solution to the problem, but I would sure like to be one again.

(81) Old age

There always have been a lot of old people wandering around, but today they seem to be everywhere. People of young age generally perceive these people as being apart from what is happening. They are out of their thoughts almost entirely other than when necessary to associate with them at family gatherings. I will be the first to admit that people of my generation had much less interaction with old people than young people do today due to our vast numbers. Of course those were the days when parents raised their children and the grandparents were not involved. It is, and was, uncomfortable being around old people because they are so old fashioned and have little knowledge of anything a young person would like to discuss. And now, young people perceive old people as being a drain on society and they will have to foot the bill. Old people are just getting in the way. They don't have to work, and the ones they see who have money, it is kind of a waste.

Now that some of us are old people, we see a lot more old people than when we were young and we have a different perception of old people. We think that the guy who coined the phrase, "The golden years" ought to be dragged out and shot. After you reach retirement age is when the work begins, as well as the depletion of any wealth you may have. Old people who are not very wealthy live a day away from financial devastation. Genetically you are supposed to be dead by the time you hit fifty and your body knows it, and so does the medical profession. For us old people, that is just when we *started* dying. Technology keeps us alive well beyond our historical life expectancy. The more old people we know, the more people we know who are having medical issues and that is just about all of them. So there are the dead and dying surrounding you. Illness is the prominent topic of discussion among older people and can be somewhat depressing and you don't hear a lot of discussion pertaining to long range planning for obvious reasons. Due to our extended life expectancy, The Golden Years usually involves caring for a parent well beyond the golden years and requires several to care for one. The financial aspects of old age for people who are not wealthy is a disaster. Due to the numbers of old people who are not wealthy, without Medicare and Medicaid in place, our society would collapse. Those who advocate eliminating these programs have not given the matter enough thought. If everyone who is dependent on these programs today were cut off from them, it would be devastating for the generation beneath them and consequently the next generation as well as the next. The only winners would be the wealthy in a nation of people being financially devastated, and this scenario seldom works out well for the wealthy. It is called the redistribution of wealth the hard way.

The stress level among the old is right up there, due to waiting for their turn to pass on and all of the loved ones falling around them. Good news is a rare thing. Not only that, you lose your hair, teeth, hearing, eyesight, taste, and things just aren't as much fun as they used to be. It is not a pretty picture, but old people make the best of it. There is a lot of thought to be given by people who save their money during the years they could enjoy themselves so they can retire at 65 and enjoy The Golden Years.

(82) What do we owe future generations?

This question is kicked around due to our national debt, which is passed from generation to generation. Some perceive this debt as unfair to future generations as they will be burdened with paying off this debt. Therefore we owe our grandchildren a national debt of $0.00.

My perception is that we should do what we can to decrease the national debt, but not make the situation worse attempting to do so. As to what we owe them, we owe them nothing. Everything that exists when the generations arrive is part of that debt. Was a lot of the debt due to wasteful spending? Why certainly. Was a lot of it spent so they have the luxury of even being born? Yes. Was the amount wasted something that the next generations won't be guilty of also? Not a chance. On the other hand, as I believe we can start decreasing the debt in a matter of months if we want to, we might as well just do it. Not for the sake of future generations, but because we can. The rest of the world may go to hell and drag us with them, but we will get there debt free.

(83) Illegal drugs

I don't know who is more pathetic, the drug dealers or the drug consumers. There would be no drug cartels, dealers and fewer illegal immigrants if there were not a vast number of drug consumers in the U.S. It is pretty convincing to me that drug trafficking is unstoppable by today's methods. In reality, drug trafficking, cartels, dealers, as well as drugs being consumed within the U.S. could be stopped completely in two months. There are two methods, which will solve the problem immediately. The first is that when loads of illegal drugs are discovered, just poison them and let them pass. The second is to develop a chemical compound that can be added to illegal drugs, which makes the consumer violently ill. In two months, multibillion dollar expenses stop and untold misery, crime, social problems, prison populations decrease, and so on. Now this is what I call a war on drugs. I am fully aware of the social and international ramifications of the first method, but if we can put a man on the moon we certainly have the medical technology to introduce method two.

Am I the first person to think of this? I doubt it. Have you heard anyone of high authority suggest either plan, I doubt that too. Why is that? The first method is out of the question if known to the public because of the moral implications and how many politicians, lawyers, doctors, businessmen, students, children, workers, and criminals could we afford to lose in two weeks. This would totally disrupt our society. The second method, which is not unknown to the medical field for some addictions, would also affect the same people, but so be it. As it is an illegal activity, which indicates a penalty, I think throwing up in the toilet stool every time a drug is used is justified. If there are a few fatalities to this illness, well, there are a few drug overdose fatalities daily anyway.

(84) Iran

Iranian leaders are on the threshold of making the same mistake as a lot of Middle Eastern leaders have made. The leaders believe they are following the will of God and they are severely underestimating the consequences of their actions. It is a waiting game for their enemies. The game being that the world is waiting for the people of Iran to discover the consequences of their leader's actions before the leaders do something stupid, and the citizens put a stop to it. If the Iranian citizens do not stop it, *someone will put a stop to it.* As soon as they are considered an imminent threat to any number of different countries, they will be toast. There may be a lot of collateral damage and it may start the religious war, which is already under way, but they will all be toast then. Like people all over the world, the Iranian leaders do not give enough thought to consequences of actions. My perception of Iranian citizens is that they are generally an intelligent and progressive people who are not unreasonable by nature, but they are brain locked by their religion and the religious leaders of that country. The leader of Iran who is prone to comparing others to Hitler is leading his people down the same path that Hitler took.

(85) How you go through life

There are three ways to go through life. The first is; you can go through life with the attitude that you are always right and don't know that you are not. What is in your best interest is your primary concern and you should acquire as much as you can while you can. You judge everyone by what they have, as it is an indicator of their worthiness. You are an opportunist as that is the best way to serve your best interest.

The second is that you can go through life with the attitude that you could acquire more than you need at the loss of other time and effort you would rather spend with family and friends, your natural surroundings and your personal interests in life. You do not have to have a new truck every three years and you pursue and enjoy things that the group number one people do not have time for. You know what your responsibilities are and you fulfill these and not at the expense of someone else. You understand that all people have their issues and you deal with them accordingly.

Group number three are the people who do not seem to have a sense of responsibility and personal pride. They take advantage of group's number one and two and want to be like group number one. To do this, there is always a scheme or a get rich quick method that they are going to perform, but never seem to get around to it or pull it off. They are not satisfied with what they have and think groups one and two should help them out. But, the help is never enough and there is always another time they need help.

In defense of group number three; there may be reasons they are in group number three, which are out of their control. There are many social, physical and mental issues which put them in group number three and they are just trying to survive.

My perception of the three groups is that the group number two people are the most admirable. They would like to have what group number one has, but wouldn't do it to get it. Group number one people have it, but can see that it was at the expense of what the group number two people had. Group number one people eventually try to act like group number two people, but it is too late.

Group number three people are pissed at groups numbers one and two because they never had what either group had.

Like with everything, there is a gray area between groups one, two and three. These two gray areas may well be the best place to spend your life as it requires the understanding of the problems of each group and the ability to interact with them

(86) Immigration and illegal aliens from Mexico

In response to a pass along email that was critical of Mexican illegal aliens and the expense incurred by the U.S. to this problem, I responded to my friends email and he then responded to my reply. While acknowledging the seriousness of the issue, I was just giving him my perception of the issue and he in turn gave me his. The result was a rational discussion of the problem without hate, prejudice and political rhetoric.

When I use the term Mexicans, they could be Mexican Americans or illegal aliens from Mexico.

My letter starts, and is how I perceive the problem.

Hey partner,

I have been giving the immigration thing some thought. Before the immigration thing though, what I remember of Mexican and U.S. history has some bearing on this issue from the point of view of Hispanics in the U.S.

The Mexican border use to be in Oregon and Mexico included the areas of now Arizona, California, New Mexico, Nevada, Utah and part of Texas. Under questionable circumstances, and I will leave it to you to research why Mexico would give up half their country, a new border was designated where the border is today.

When this was done, the U.S. government agreed that every Mexican National north of the new border could go south or remain as U.S. citizens. Any Mexican National who owned land above the border could keep it as personal property. It's been a while, but the number 80,000 Mexicans rings a bell, which is probably close due to all of the Hispanic named towns and cities in the west. I don't know the year and too lazy to look, but in the eighteen hundreds.

Just as a note of trivia. We are aware of all of the U.S. Calvary posts in the southwest. Not commonly known, but most of these forts and patrols were not established to protect the white immigrants from the Indians or the whites from the new Hispanic Americans. They were positioned in the southwest to protect the new Hispanic Americans from the Indians who had a campaign of genocide going on against these Hispanics.

Anyway, 80,000 new Hispanic U.S. citizens makes one wonder how many that has multiplied into since that time. No telling how many millions.

Again, the U.S. said that any Mexican owning property north of the new border would retain it as personal property. After the new border was established and the new Hispanic U.S. citizen landowners settled in, a problem arose when a white U.S. citizen took a liking to a piece of land owned by a Hispanic. When this happened, the government would tell the Hispanic landowner to present proof of ownership. As we Americans had almost exclusively granted Homesteads in the west, the Mexicans were awarded Land Grants by whatever government or Country was in control of Mexico at the time. Most of these were registered in towns and churches now in the U.S. and due to fires and other mysterious problems, these documents disappeared.

Documents from Mexico were in almost every case disallowed for various reasons. Only a few of the 80,000 were able to keep their land. The U.S. was doing to them what they had been doing to the America Indians for years as a matter of policy. I would guess that a lot of the 80,000 went back south as there was no point being in the U.S. as there was no work for them and the Indians were raising hell with them. This is just background info in an attempt to understand the thought process of the Hispanic Americans up until today.

As for the immigration problem. We should by now know who started this problem. It was the agricultural community and anyone who financially benefited from agricultural profits. Without researching the matter specifically, I am guessing that this started around 1938 or so because before that they had Okies running out of their ears from the dust bowl and they were not treating them all that well. Anyway, the Mexicans would work for even less that the Okies. When the Second World War started, the entire agricultural workforce became Hispanics, whether U.S. citizens or from across the border. It was soon discovered that Mexican Nationals bitched less about how little they were making than the U.S. Hispanics. Farmers would send truck convoys to Mexico to bring them up here to work. I don't know what the immigration laws were at the time, but I get a big picture of two border patrol guards waving them through. The new dams and irrigation projects and the new farms required thousands of illegal Mexicans. Everybody knew it and there was not a peep from anybody. It seems that there never was a problem with the illegals until drugs and related violence became part of the equation. With the drugs, came the criminals, the gangs, the violence and the occupation of large sections of the cities.

Then everybody looked around and said, My God, look how many Mexicans there are. But you still don't hear the private sector who utilizes Mexican labor bitching. Their big problem has always been, how to get away with it. Now that everyone is aware of the problem and some immigration laws are enforced, there is the problem of what do we do with all of the illegals, which the private sector would just love to keep employing. Now we have a lot of illegals that can't work unless they have a false I.D., which has also been fine with the private sector. The criminal Mexican element and the gangs have found a very lucrative business in the U.S., and never accuse the Hispanics of being dumb. In six months they can learn English and we can't learn Spanish at all unless we go to college for years. This being the case, they take advantage of every social program we have. Hell, we have generation after generation of Americans doing the same thing, so it is hypocritical to blame them for playing the system, but **we can blame them** for being illegals and doing it. All U.S. citizens are to blame to various degrees as we all saw it happening, we all took advantage of lower prices due to the low wages paid and we said nothing until it was a problem. I never gave it much thought until like everyone else; I became aware of the criminal and social program problems. Living in an area which had little problems with Mexicans other than the few killings in the area and they were almost always killing each other, was probably my reason for lack of concern.

My ignorance and perceptions are based on daily living where I see a lot of Mexicans working and very few white people working. Assuming these are not illegals, they seem to be extraordinarily hard workers and have a hell of a lot better attitude than others doing the same job. I have an email pal in Mexico who I worked with when he was an illegal and I was not aware of it. I worked with him for two years and when I was taking him to see my mother, he said he could not go in the house and see her because he was an illegal alien and he had not told me. I told him I didn't care if he was purple and I have two white guys working for me that I would trade for him. (Guilty) He moved back to Mexico because his wife didn't like it up here.

I rented a house to a Mexican couple who worked in another city. I asked the gal why she wanted to live here when they both worked in the other city? She said she had two kids and she did not want them going to school with the Mexicans in the other city. She was afraid of the gang situation.

It was then I realized that not only do **we** have a problem with the Mexicans; they have a problem with them too.

I am sorry to say that we now have a Hispanic based economy. Go anywhere, the Mexicans are working and they buy shopping carts full of clothes, TVs' and groceries. The Mall and Granny's, is like going to Mexico City. Almost our entire agricultural production is Mexican labor. Oh yeah, let's not forget, that is where we can get our recreational drugs.

Ok, there are millions of U.S. Hispanic citizens above the border. Millions of illegal aliens and more are coming aboard every day. Prisons full of criminals from both groups, which is just like us going to college. I think we can safely say that the criminal element and those involved in gangs in the U.S., although disgusting, is a different issue than the illegal alien worker issue.

The illegal alien and immigration problem is a complex problem and knee jerk solutions are easy to say, but like everything else it is much more complex than the knee jerk solutions we hear on a daily basis. To stop illegals crossing the border in my opinion is probably not a possibility.

Some of my reasons for saying this are;

The Mexican/ U.S. border is 1954 miles long.

We presently have 697 miles of border, which is presently only experiencing limited illegal alien crossings.

This presently requires 17,399 border patrol personnel and this is the easiest part of the border, close to housing and so on for the guards and their families.

The remaining 1257 miles not adequately controlled would require approximately an additional 35,000 border patrol personnel which would bring us to about 53,000 border patrol personnel, all their trucks, helicopters, sensor devices, arms, living facilities, gasoline, etc, etc. This amounts to an entire army.

I would guess the annual expense would go from the now 10.1 billion dollars to around 40 billion dollars. After we catch them we have to spend another 10 billion to get them back to Mexico. Those we put in jail would be very expensive, another five billion.

I don't think that U.S. citizens could stomach a 53,000 man army and $55,000,000,000.00 a year to stop the problem we have with illegal aliens.

We also have to bear in mind that we only have 32 secure miles of Canadian border. This brings up a whole new bunch of possibilities if a Mexican wants to get into the U.S. Then what?

After we have the 53,000 guards at the border, the aliens stop. Then what again? We leave; they are back coming across the border.

I could not help running into the U.S. vs. Arizona lawsuit controversy. 99% of the information on the Internet is why the Obama administration is screwing up again. This being the case, I had to look long and hard for anything in defense of the lawsuit or at least an explanation or argument for the lawsuit.

I read the legislation passed by the State of Arizona a while back when I first heard about it. I have to admit that at the time I saw some real problems with it. *Of course at the time I was already pissed off about the Arizona gun dealers selling assault weapons by the hundreds and crates of ammunition when it was obvious it was all going to Mexico. Sure enough, one of our border patrol agents was killed with one of these guns. It was all legal, well who gives a damn if it was legal or not, they are as bad as the ass holes they sell them to.* On the surface, the legislation was not offensive to me, as I am a **believer** in racial profiling. If five Arabs get on the plane with me, I want them searched. The problems I saw with it is that in order to facilitate such legislation, you are going to be confronted with thousands of pissed off U.S. Mexicans when they constantly get stopped and checked for I.D. and if they don't have it, they are incarcerated or have to call for proof. The lawsuit potential is there, and there will be 10,000 ACLU lawyers clogging the courts. After reading it, I questioned its constitutionality and the problems that it might cause.

My biggest concern was the end run problem. All Arizona is doing is just creating a problem for adjacent

States. I sympathize with Arizona, but should they be sending their grief to adjacent States?

Well those were my concerns a while back. I am not certain about this but it appears that the U.S. Government's opinion on the legislation and its effects are as follows. And in layman language.

The Government says that constitutionally, the Federal Government has jurisdiction over immigration into the United States. The State of Arizona has exceeded its authority. This Arizona legislation which is in contrast with federal jurisdiction will create a burden on the Federal Government. To facilitate such State regulations will require resources by the Federal Government from the current immigration laws, resource management, and enforcement. Whereas the Federal Government places a priority on the safety of the Nation from terrorists and aliens from specific terrorist prone countries, this would reduce their resources to do this if the emphasis is on the many Latin America aliens.

Whereas the State of Arizona contends that it has the Constitutional right because they are just enforcing the present Federal immigration laws. Which could well be true. Not being a constitutional lawyer, I cannot say who is correct. The Attorney General of Arizona was fired or threatened to be fired by the Arizona Governor because he said he would not defend the legislation. Which means the legislation is either unconstitutional, he is a Democrat, or is looking for a job with the Feds.

My gut feeling is that unless the State of Arizona legislation is the same as other adjacent States, it is not the right thing to do. With California as an adjoining state, that doesn't seem likely. They would have a Watts x 10 situation on their hands.

Legislation as passed by Arizona could never be passed by the U.S. Congress, as it would have the smell of a police state, as well as a possible twenty million-citizen revolt on their hands.

Lastly, lethal force at the border could eliminate this illegal alien problem, but that would have tremendous repercussions, as lethal force would be on the table for everyone involved and worldwide condemnation.

I know I have over thought this topic, but that's just me.

Tom

P.S. I love being criticized, so tell me what's wrong with my conclusions.

My friend's gracious reply was as follows.

Tom

As usual you have given all this a great deal of thought. After spending Jan and Feb in Tucson AZ trying to run from old man winter I had to do some adjustments in my thinking about the immigration thing. I came face to face with some past US - Mexican history. The whole Southwest is highly Hispanic.

My first gut reaction, (usually wrong) was to just give the Mexicans the state of California as a concession. Possession is 9/10 of the law. Like you mentioned, most of the Southwest was their territory in the first place. They are just trying to take back what they think is their land in the first place. The US - Mexican war, 1845-1848 makes me think that we stole this land from them anyway. In that regard, I am sympathetic towards their cause. Maybe we should just try to re-negotiate some kind of settlement or peace accord. Does this sound like the Israel/Palestine issue?

Also like you, my problem is the legal question. If they are here Illegal, they are breaking the law and should be prosecuted in some manner. The government is afraid of enforcing the law. As you mentioned, my gut feeling is that unless the State of Arizona legislation is the same as other adjoining States, it is not the right thing to do. With California as an adjoining state, that doesn't seem likely. They would have a Watts x 10 situation on their hands."

If the law is an unfair law, then it should be changed. Do we have the political will to do this? What is the will of the people on this matter? We have become such a fragmented society that we can't even reach a consensus of opinion on this matter. I can't say that we have great leaders in our country but again, like you have said in the past, it is we who keep them in office. We vote them in.

I certainly agree with your statement "Legislation as passed by Arizona could never be passed by the U.S. Congress as it would have the smell of a police state, as well as a possible 20 million citizen revolt on their hands."

This is no simple matter to solve; however we have several "Think Tank" institutions that we could be getting some good ideas from. I think it boils down to the political will to solve this problem among a fractured political diverse population. Even if it means political suicide for any politician brave enough to present some decent proposals.

Your partner

(87) Yard sales

Now here is a topic that will make some people cringe and others get up before daylight Saturday morning. Yard sale people are usually fanatical in their pursuit. They will bail out of their car and leave it in the middle of the street to

173

beat the next guy to the accumulation of what at least one person and everyone before them does not want. Yard sale arrivals are planned like a military campaign. The enemy is located by reconnaissance. The location is mapped and the location is hit in the quickest possible manner considering there are closer targets that have to be hit first.

When at the target, they are confronted with two types of sellers. Those who have things of little use or they do not need anymore, or people just like themselves who had bought the stuff the week before at a yard sale. The person who just doesn't want something any more puts a ridiculously low price on it to get rid of it and not have to haul it to Goodwill. He is asking fifty cents for something he paid fourteen dollars for. The out of breath customer offers him twenty-five cents. *My God, I cringe at the thought of the humiliating offer. If it is worth twenty-five cents it sure as hell must be worth fifty cents and you wouldn't have to make an ass out of yourself.* The seller is usually too embarrassed to argue over a quarter. The customer in a state of euphoria gets the item to the middle of the street where the car is and speeds away to the next target.

His next target is the person just like him. The price on a similar object is fifty cents because this guy embarrassed a seller last week and got it for a quarter. The customer says he just bought one for a quarter and the seller says that next week at the big flea market he can get two dollars for it. The customer thinks, "If he can get two dollars for it at the flea market so can I", and buys it for fifty cents."

Sunday morning at the flea market there are four hundred tables set up and loaded with material that they had all bought in the past. It turns out that the only people at the flea market are the vendors. The vendors all walk around and look at each other's stuff and look at the prices, which they know are retail prices and they can't make any money buying at retail prices, so nobody buys anything. They have been there since 4:00 AM and now the temperature is either 110 degrees or there is a dust storm. They all start slowly folding up and leaving and talking to their spouse about the guy that found a Picasso painting at a yard sale in Georgia. Next Saturday they are back in action on the battlefield and they do not find a Picasso, but they do find some things they have to buy because they can get them ridiculously cheap. As for me, if I asked ten cents for something and the guy offered me a nickel, I would slap him or just break it in front of him.

Oh yeah, the first guy that just wanted to get rid of the stuff and spent all day Friday setting it up and marking prices, made $13.25 before it started the downpour.

(88) Terrorism

In this topic, I am only referring to Muslim terrorism, although there are many others. My perception of Muslim terrorism and how to survive it is as follows. Muslim terrorists are extremely few in numbers, which is the primary problem of fighting them. The militant members within the Muslim community are primarily the extremists. In the field in large numbers they would not be considered as terrorists, but as insurgents and represent a much larger target which can be located and confronted. Muslim terrorists on the other hand are smaller groups or cells and don't necessarily have the same ideology as ordinary militant Muslims. The philosophy of the Muslim terrorists is such that they have few mental weaknesses and there are no terrorists you can negotiate with. How do you deal with an individual who believes that death in pursuit of killing their enemy (being us) is a pleasurable and honorable religious event? This has been taught since birth and everyone in their world agrees with them.

The only way to defeat this type of terrorism is for the terrorists to decide not to participate in the activity. If this is not obtainable it cannot be defeated, but can only be interrupted or stopped on a single event basis. When one dies, there is always a replacement available. There is something being done or something the terrorist organizations are afraid of or there would be a hundred terrorist acts a day, not one every so often. I suspect what they are afraid of must be reprisals. I think the Jews are aware of this and act accordingly. A paradox is that the people who seem to have the least respect for life are also the ones who wail the loudest at the death of a Martyr. What they fear the most is being killed in a setting where they will not be recognized as a Martyr, but just as a dead Muslim. A militant Muslin not killed behind enemy lines or making the supreme sacrifice cannot count on being a Martyr. It seems that the Muslim community must be aware of the act and then proclaim him as a Martyr.

The U.S. is doing an excellent job with the drones in this respect and it has really gotten their attention. One thing which we as the enemy should know by this time, is that the Muslims are not a significant fighting force as an army. The Republican Guard as well as our apparent inability to train an Iraq or Afghan army is testament to this, as well as was the Six-Day War against Israel.

I cannot think of any more than what we are currently doing to combat terrorism, but it appears to me that they are susceptible to constant pressure and the liquidation of every new leader who steps to the plate.

(89) An apology to bass fishermen (on the lighter side)

I have recently concluded that the scale of intelligence of living creatures has been wrong, as humans were at the top of this scale. Examining all of the facts, this will have to be changed and the largemouth bass should be just above humans. This has to be true because humans cannot outsmart the largemouth bass. The bass has been studied for a hundred years by thousands of people as to every aspect of their behavior and we still cannot determine what it would prefer to eat. Anglers try to use the preferred food mimic of the bass, but every year a hundred new better lures are discovered. It seems that humans do not have the mental capacity to determine which one is the best. In the human's defense, there is the possibility that the bass are evolving extremely rapidly. So fast that we cannot keep up with their preferred food. They are so smart that they even have a preferred reel type on the other end of the fishing line and that changes all of the time. The solution to this problem is not to produce the best lure, reel and line for this time, but figure out what they will like a month from now and finally outsmart them.

(90) School teachers

Teaching school is an occupation or job like any other. My reason for selecting school teachers as a topic is that everyone is absolutely familiar with this occupation. I have a perception of school teachers which is based on my own experience. I suppose teachers in New York may be different than those in San Francisco, but I can't address that possibility. My experience at the time was that most grade school teachers were women. The women teachers were by far the better teachers in respect that it was obvious that the women seemed to have a social link to the students and this is probably because by nature women rear children and teach them. The men teachers seemed to have an air of mental superiority about them, which was all too obvious to the students. This idiosyncrasy prevailed all of the way through high school and is more pronounced in the higher grades, with the exception of the men teachers who obviously did not care or even want to be there. They were waiting for the end of the day just like the students.

The women still out shined the men in the higher grades, as it appeared they had the attitude that teaching was their profession and that was what they were there for. This is a little critical, and was not true in every case, but men teachers had a tendency to take advantage of a captive audience. It was not long until you knew a lot about his personal life, what he liked and did not like, his personal experiences, news of the day, where he went to college, and many personal stories. This was great for the students to pass the time, but resulted in more homework, to be graded by the student next to you, whereas the women teachers usually took your work and personally graded it. If the male teacher was a sports coach, the situation was almost unbearable. Their air of superiority was greatly enhanced and the athletes were the only ones he would associate with. He usually had to leave class early for practice or something. It was obvious that the class he was teaching was very secondary to his coaching job.

Other students may have a different perception, as I was always the kid that showed up to class with no pencil or paper and had left my schoolbooks at home or I had lost them.

(91) Natural disasters

Natural disasters as I understand them, apply to Earth origin events that effect the human population. If people were not on the Earth, they would probably be called extreme environmental events. This being the case, a natural disaster is simply caused by people being in a location where they should not have been when the environmental event happened. We have earthquakes, tornadoes, hurricanes, floods, tsunamis, avalanches, volcanic eruptions and many more environmental events which we have concluded with no doubt, were going to occur. It is not a matter of if, but when. These events will be natural disasters because people have made a choice to be there if the event happens in their lifetime. Some of these events happen much more frequently than others, but that seems to make little difference to the population. It almost appears that they bunch up in areas where these events are going to take place. There are many reasons people seek residence in these areas, and in respect to the danger of natural disasters; they appear to be in a state of denial.

Having lived all of my life in an area that is almost void of natural disaster potential, I marvel at the people who live in Tornado Alley and the Gulf States ravaged by hurricanes. This is to say nothing of the people who live along the Mississippi drainage system on the flood plain. People can't seem to build enough structures on the San Andreas Fault and the people living on the Pacific Ocean coastline at lower elevations are in a perilous situation.

There is a mental perception by people that the longer it has been since it previously happened, the safer they are. In reality the opposite is the truth and they are just getting closer to the next event.

The San Andreas Fault is two tectonic plates sliding by one another and they have been doing this for thousands of years. This fault creates earthquakes that can be devastating. Scientists cannot predict when the next one will occur, but they do know the frequency of the earthquakes in the past. There is a pattern to their frequency and as like all other things, we are overdue for the big one. The rational thing to do would be to get out of the path of the disaster, but this is not happening. Although some of the people in California joke about the situation, they are highly aware of it and I think they are confined to that area due to financial situations such as their job or business. I refuse to believe they are not nervous about the situation. On top of that, there are hundreds of thousands of them who are in double jeopardy due to associated or unrelated Tsunamis. Off shore faults or landslides in the Hawaiian Islands will devastate the low-lying areas as high as 500 feet above sea level along the Pacific Ocean coastline. Most are aware of the earthquakes and small tsunamis, but few are aware of the Hawaiian connection, being the big one. Up the coast further north are many low lying cities including Portland, and Seattle who are in a perilous situation due to the faults off the west coast and again the Hawaiian connection which would pretty well take the cities out.

The Hawaiian landslides have happened in the past and there is conclusive evidence that another is inevitable. The geological factors required for the slides are already beginning to happen. The latest big Tsunami that hit Japan should be an eye opener to people on the West Coast. FEMA is aware of the situation and has already made some arrangements for the aftermath of such a catastrophe, but they are not advertising the arrangements.

The continuous tornado, hurricane and flood disasters in the southern and eastern U.S. are endured, and people rebuild on the same house foundation. Denial seems to lose its appeal after continuous events and some move out of harm's way, but their choices of relocation are usually in the path of another pending natural environmental event.

After saying, "I would not live in that hell forsaken place," I look around at the situation I have lived with for 60 years. Although this area is void of natural environmental events, I have been sitting in an area that is very susceptible to manmade disasters. I have been living below many huge dams susceptible to the domino effect, poison gas storage areas, nuclear reactors, LNG storage areas, etc.

The bottom line is that I have the option of moving to another location, but have not and will not. My perception of the hazardous comparison of my situation to the others I have mentioned is that it is safer, because these events are extremely rare, but there is no assurance they will not happen. Being a fatalist at heart, I have considered my options if an event occurs and have a rudimentary plan, but it has a lot of holes in it.

For the all of the factors listed above, I think that all new structures should have Safe Rooms built into them. The investment would be minimal and the lives saved could be in the thousands due to any of the events.

(92) Crime, the citizenry and personal protection.

To start, and to the great satisfaction of many of my friends, I believe that every household should have arms as personal protection against the criminal element. If need be a tyrannical government or a state of anarchy.

Unlike most others who advocate this policy and have an agenda for advocating it, I am a believer in some form of gun control. The unmentionable *gun control*, which the very mention of seems to infuriate some people to the point that the veins on their neck are sticking out. These people are exactly the reason we should have gun control. Some people hunt with guns, some collect guns, some sell guns, some are waiting to converge on the Whitehouse with guns, some are obsessed with guns, some have a feeling of power with guns, and so on. Several organizations have utilized propaganda to blow the gun control problem completely out of proportion and they have many willing followers to believe anything they say. The right to bear arms under the Constitution is ambiguous as to the right of a private citizen to bear arms unless he is a member of the militia. I suspect that was the intent, as it was not even questioned that private citizens would have guns for food and protection from savages. This is really a mute point, as all of us can become a member of a militia, as it is not an official military organization and all of us citizens would step to the plate in case of a national emergency. Before addressing the crime issue, I would just say that we have had comprehensive gun control in this country for eighty years with no detrimental effects, so the term *gun control* should not be that shocking. I never anticipate a time when I will not have a gun capable of self-protection in my home. Admittedly it may not be a fully automatic weapon with a fifty round clip, but it will do the job.

Crime against the citizenry of this country appears to be proportional to the chances of getting caught. If every crime was detected and the perpetrators punished, there would be very little to no crime against the citizenry. Crime in New York City went from ramped to almost none when they instituted a *policeman on every corner* tactic. Of course there was little crime by criminals and increased crime by the policemen, but that was out of sight with considerably less bloodshed.

Our best weapon in the war against crime is surveillance. Criminals hate surveillance, as they know they will probably get caught and punished. As the police do not have the resources for total surveillance, it is the job of the citizenry to help in that respect. Block watches, security systems, video monitoring of homes and businesses are all a detriment to criminal acts. Of course the residents of a home who are armed is in itself quite an impediment to crimes. Surveillance in association with the police is a formidable enemy to the criminally inclined.

As violent acts against citizens are everyone's largest concern and the numbers of law enforcement officers is the best defense against this, I cannot imagine the ordinary citizen agreeing to cut the budget of law enforcement. Our taxes pay for law enforcement and I am more than willing to pay more taxes for increased protection. I am also willing to pay additional taxes to law enforcement agencies to ride herd on the gangs that have developed, and I don't think I am different than anyone else in this respect. Of course I do not live in a gated community with private security as some do and I think maybe these people are the ones who would cut law enforcement and hang us out to dry.

This is not an ideological or political problem; it's a personal problem when you are looking into the muzzle of a gun.

Crimes of passion, sex crimes and crimes such as committed in a state of rage, are not preventable, as the perpetrators have lost reasoning at that point. We have to live with these possibilities and protect ourselves accordingly.

(93) My reply to an email about *more poor Democrats than poor Republicans*

And that is the way it will always be. The poor will usually vote for Democrats and the rich will usually vote for Republicans. Why is this? Is there something the Democrats know that the Republicans don't? Is there something the Republicans know that the Democrats don't?

Ironically the answer to this is; **Yes.** There are a variety of reasons and one being that both groups are wearing different colored glasses. No matter what they see it is the shade of their colored glasses. Very few social matters are black and white in nature. A good Democrat or Republican will never try to contradict their own beliefs by investigation, rational thought or logic. One might equate this to asking a devout Christian to read the Koran and he says, "There is no point in it." But in contrast to that, you can bet our best generals have read the Koran for obvious reasons.

Another obvious reason that the poor will vote for a Democrat is because they think they or the U.S. will be

better off. The same applies for the rich and the
Republicans.

Fundamentally this implies that the poor Democrats believe
they would be less poor and the rich Republicans believe
they would be more rich. The implications of either of the
scenario can be significant.

At present, it is not obvious to me that the poor, like the
rich, give much thought to anything but what is in their self
interest.

As this subject matter refers to the poor and Democrats
and the rich and Republicans, this leaves out the middle
income group. If you convince one of these that they can
also be rich, they will surely vote Republican. If you can
convince one of these that they will eventually be poor, they
will vote for a Democrat.

The middle income group is the group which is the
most reasonable and logical when it comes to self-interest.
They could go either way depending on this self-interest
motivation. As well, the best of Socialist Liberals wants his
financial position assured before he works on anyone else's.

What troubles me is that if you are not wearing either
color of glasses, you are getting a depressing feeling in
respect to a lot of Americans. In this age of electronic
communication and commercial enterprises and practices,
we have developed a culture similar to a lot of other less
moral cultures and countries around the world. In my youth
I was taught that to lie was a sin. Not only that, if you were
caught in a lie you were disgraced and there was a loss of
personal integrity and Jesus was not happy with you. In our
present society and culture, lying has become acceptable
practice. In the commercial sector, there is a massive
amount of lying going on whether by used car salesmen or

bankers or mortgage companies. I think we have seen enough evidence of this. Lying at Congressional hearings on TV before the world, no problem. Lying, half-truths, words out of context, cherry picked quotes and $3.99.9 works.

I have received hundreds of emails which fit into this category. Having laboriously checked hundreds of these emails for accuracy, my numbers are that 90% fall into these non-credible categories. I guess that is why I got the email in the first place. If it is not a good public argument on its own merit, just spin it a little. All of this effort by myself is just because I don't have a pair of those damned colored glasses.

I have to admit that I am starting to get a hint of color, which can be attributed to a backlash to the sources and content of information I am receiving and seeing on television.

I hesitate to judge others due to my lack of knowledge about them. As well, I want no one judging me, because they surely do not know me well enough. I am not without opinion of some of the wackos in politics that I have watched, and their mental prowess, but it is surely just an opinion on my part because millions of people (with the glasses) bought the program.

Obama was voted into office as President of the U.S. Do I support him? Yes, but not blindly. If McCain had been voted in I would do the same. This is a Democratic Republic and that is what we as Americans are supposed to do. Do you have to like them, their race, religion and social philosophy? No. But as a citizen you have the moral responsibility to the guys on Omaha beach to honor the office until the President is voted out of office or impeached. Being a black Democrat is not yet grounds for impeachment, so that is what I will do. If I don't like four years of Obama, I will vote against him. I didn't vote for him the first time, so I don't have to try to save face   .

The lying, spinning of facts and all of the other bullshit that is going on is an embarrassment for me. We as Americans should be above that, and the good the bad and the ugly should be judged on its own merit. If everyone is buying what the news commentators are preaching, why don't we just vote one of them into office? They are the ones that have all of the world problem solving answers.

Will we be better off after another two years if a Republican is voted President instead of a Democrat? Hell, I don't know and nobody else does either. I cannot foresee into the future. Of course I don't have the colored glasses on, but if I did, I would simply say, "Yes" or "No", as careful examination of the topic would have no point. I can't go through life second-guessing every conceivable event that can happen in two years, I have the same real good hindsight as everyone else, but without the colored glasses.

(94) Why stimulus bills do not work.

It is true that an economic situation can arise in the U.S. that requires money to be pumped into the economy. The term, *Stimulus* implies the intent, in that the money is supposed to stimulate the economy.   When the situation arises and stimulus money is pumped into the society, it does not seem to do everything necessary to stimulate the economy. The economy notices the influx of money and reacts to it, but it does not have any long-term effect. When the money runs out, you are right back where you started. It is true that jobs are created, but they last the life of the stimulus money. This is not necessarily a bad thing because

TOM NORTON

this could stop a recession which is out of control and buys a little time. In fact, that is all stimulus money has done is buy time. Unless stimulus money creates a manufacturing base and assures a market for manufactured goods, it is just a band-aid on a heart attack.

What happens to stimulus package money? It goes to many different recipients. The States receive money to prevent the layoff of employees and be able to sustain necessary services, it extends unemployment benefits, it creates temporary jobs, it goes to the citizens to pay bills and of course some goes to recipients who do not need it. If our recent stimulus packages had worked, the U.S. would have received all of the stimulus money back in tax revenue, which has not been the case.

(95) Another thought on government spending.

I keep hearing that the government has to manage and balance their budget just like American families do. This is ironic in that families (excluding the wealthy again) are terrible at what they are supposed to be so good at. Credit cards at 12% interest, home mortgages, student loan payments, new vehicles, boats, cell phone contracts, and many more contracted expenses are hanging over their heads. A hiccup, loss of job, illness, divorces and for many other reasons, this can come crashing down on their heads. In fact the U.S. citizen's managing of their finances and how they have spent and obligated their money is a major player in how we ended up in this mess.

In the family's defense, this is not a cash basis world. If it were, this country would be far from the financial giant that it is. We would still have mom and pop businesses and be riding bicycles.

The government is no worse or no better than American families in respect to spending and budgets.

(96) Why is the U.S. government bailing out financial institutions and corporations?

The answer to that is, they have no choice. Those who have little knowledge of the situation or consequences blurt out, just let them go bankrupt. Oh, how the government wishes they could. But there are stumbling blocks which have to do with losing what little industry we have left in this country, increased imports, imminent property foreclosures, increased unemployment, imminent losses to individuals, stock market crashes (domestic and international), imminent recessions, etc.

For the most part, historically and playing out today, bailouts have resulted in only acceptable losses to the government. In a lot of cases the government has made money on these bailouts. I might add that a good portion of the private sector has thanked the U.S. Government and the taxpayers for these bailouts by continuing their same old questionable policies of increased bonuses and stock options to the elite personnel in the institutions and corporations. We keep hearing that if they don't pay the CEO a twenty million dollar bonus, they will lose him. Not only do I highly doubt that, I suspect there are hundreds of people out there, as, or more knowledgeable, who would gladly do the job for a mere ten million. I think there are cigar smoke filled rooms all over America with people laughing their asses off at us taxpayers, stock holders and customers.

(97) The private sector and private enterprise and how they work

My perception of how private enterprise works is as follows. A successful private enterprise is where you have a product or service for which you receive more money than your expenses to furnish the goods or services. In the case of goods, you pay less for them, or to have them manufactured for less than a purchaser will pay for them. As for services, when goods are included the same applies, but services are labor intensive and the purchaser will pay the equivalent to higher labor costs than the service provider is paying. The bottom line to this scenario and the end result is called profit.

As profit is the motivating factor of the private sector and private enterprise, it is safe to conclude that the more profit you make, the more you have satisfied your quest. There are many ways to increase profits. You sell more goods and services, increase your prices, reduce your costs, relocate, etc.

Now one must take into consideration the reality of the situation, being that business enterprises are not a friend of their costs, which includes labor. They are also not a friend of each other, being competitors, and they are not a friend of the Internal Revenue Service or the purchasers of their goods and services. The object being profit, these are enemies they have to contend with.

Without interjecting my personal feelings on any of these matters, but just my perception as to how private enterprise and the private sector works, is as follows:

Labor costs have always been an important issue with business enterprises because it is a major expense and is a variable that in the past could be managed. In the seventeen hundreds, the early labor costs were a one-time expense of the price of a slave and then feeding him for the rest of his life. After the initial expense the labor costs were minimal. As only the wealthy could afford the price of a slave, this quickly eliminated the competition of any non-slave owners and large plantations were the end result. Life was good for private enterprise, being the wealthy plantation owners. These people invested in small businesses in town and in some cases owned small towns. Life was good for business enterprises and not that good for the white population and very bad for the slave population.

After the Civil War and those who survived it, business enterprises were still doing very well as the large plantations still existed although maybe by different owners. The earlier slave population changed in many ways, but not financially. Most of the slaves stayed on at the plantations for room and board and a few as well as many poor whites became sharecroppers for the wealthy. Eventually many blacks moved north and were willing to work for less than the Irish immigrants. This was good for private enterprise and was not good for the blacks and the Irish who were at each other's throats, literally.

The eighteen hundreds was also a good time for business and private enterprise. The Intercontinental Railroad with Irish and Chinese immigrants keeping the labor costs at a very minimum. Businesses sprang up with each new town along the route with everything needed to get back all of the wages paid for construction of the railroad. For their effort, the railroads were given millions of acres of land along the route, which must have been a fantastic deal or they would never had entered into it.

The citizens in the eastern U.S., not owning businesses, loaded up in covered wagons and headed west to start a small business enterprise of their own, being a farm or ranch.

With the discovery of gold in California, many citizens could not pack their gear fast enough to get to California and most passed through the business center of San Francisco. The more unsuccessful miners there were, the more San Francisco grew, and labor costs were very favorable for all businesses. Even for the successful miners out in the field, the cost of goods increased 1000% or more just because they had to have the goods; and business was good.

On into the early twentieth century business was good. This is when the wealthy Barons were created. The mining, petroleum, steel, railroads, large ranchers, shipping, newspapers and a multitude of other businesses created a few people with vast fortunes, as well as their first tier subordinates who ran the businesses. Labor on the other hand sustained their position as being very poor. Immigrants, child labor, sweat shops, cowboys, and so on, were the norm and these people not able to save any money to get away from their employer. The business climate was good except for other competitive businesses, which commonly settled their differences by violent means.

Until the Great Depression, business was good. During the depression, the poor became poorer and now first tier employees of large businesses were jumping out of windows because they had all of their money invested in their employers company's stock when they shut the doors. For the wealthy business owners there was a loss of capital investment and a loss of income, but I don't know of any that did not weather the storm with considerable wealth. They were long term investors anyway, not day traders who are still jumping out of windows.

Business was good during the Second World War and after, although there was now a new set of circumstances.

Labor costs were not easily controlled, there was a lot of competition, and there was the curse of federal income tax to contend with. As well, you could not count on your buddies in Congress in the long term, as administrations were changing frequently and the worst of all was the government's regulation of business activities.

Although business enterprises were still successful if they worked at it, the good old days were gone.

To the present day, to be successful in business, you must have an edge over the competition. This edge takes many forms. Some of these are; Have more capital *which is the founding of corporations*, have a connection with someone who can benefit you, be more innovative, better advertisement, better locations, better tax benefits, bribery, cheaper labor, have insider information, be able to manipulate the market and the price of commodities, preferential treatment by the U.S. government, price fixing, drive your competitors out of business and so on. Without these edges, private enterprise will not work, as the competitors will destroy each other. The gas war scenario is a good example of competition alone.

Now in the history of successful business, which is what I am perceiving, the legality or lack of morality of it all, was and is, a consideration which private enterprise will push to the limit as their edge. A successful private sector and private enterprise is just that, successful regardless of how you got there.

(98) Do we need the private sector and private enterprise?

Absolutely. Without them we would be a pure socialistic society where everyone works for the government. The government would own all manufacturing and control wages and trade. It is not impossible for a pure socialistic government to own and operate everything now being done by the private sector, but the real downside to this concept is the competition factor, which is responsible for new and innovative products and competitive workers. The development of society would slow to a crawl under pure socialism and we would all be driving the same never changing model of vehicles.

Socialism can be super efficient, but this efficiency is of benefit to no one.

Money and trying to acquire more of it is what makes the world go round. It is the driving force for almost every aspect of society. It is the difference between starving and fifty-foot yachts. The only thing that makes our country work is the chance that you could someday own one of these yachts or be President of the U.S.

By the same token and repeating myself, a pure capitalistic society does not work either, so we must select the best qualities of both capitalism and socialism.

(99) Entrepreneurs

My perception of an entrepreneur is someone who already has wealth and has an edge he can use in order to accumulate more wealth. Investors with bad ideas and no edge are not entrepreneurs. Entrepreneurs make money; they do not throw it away. The thing about being a wealthy entrepreneur is that if 25% of your business ventures fail, you are still in good shape. Money has an affinity for money. If you start with a lot, you can hardly go wrong. A not so wealthy person buys $10,000.00 worth of anything and it doubles in value in ten years; he has made $10,000.00.

A wealthy person buys at $1,000,000.00 and he has made $1,000,000.00. You can say the same thing if you are drawing 10% interest on your money as many did for decades.

This reminds me of Donald Trump who started from scratch. Over $30,000,000.00 was his scratch. He has had a tumultuous business history, but you can bet he will die with considerably more than that.

(100) Unions

Having been a union member of several different unions for forty years, I have a little knowledge as to how they work. I also have a little knowledge as to the history of unions within the U.S. My perception of what a union is supposed to be and my perception of how most of them are, is two different things.

Unions originated as groups of similarly employed workers who managed to get a collective bargaining agreement with their employer or employers. This was a violent tumultuous period on both sides of the table. The intent of a union is to acquire wages and benefits they deem suitable for the job they are doing and in almost every case was more than they were presently making. This sounded so good to workers in other occupations or locations that they went through the same process. All of this had a variety of effects upon the companies that were now union affiliated. The effects ran from making the company noncompetitive, to the other extreme where work was given to them because they were union affiliated. In almost every case a union did not break a company, because the workers would lose their jobs. The unions used the technique of strikes to blackmail the company into meeting their demands, but not to the point it would result in the loss of their jobs.

In a relative short time, unions were growing in wealth due to union dues and pension funds paid by union workers. This like every other case where wealth is accumulated, it attracted people who wanted that money. In some cases unions attracted people who wanted to use their power of the strike to blackmail these companies themselves. Hence, we ended up with unions which were in collusion with organized crime or unions who were ran by someone other than the labor class and drew large wages and fringe benefits.

The sad thing about labor unions is that they started with a reasonable purpose by people only wanting a decent livable wage and that has evolved into a situation where their philosophy is now no better than the companies which caused the forming of unions. Union members think nothing of hiring professionals outside their rank and file. They have little concern or compassion for many people doing the same job they are doing for a lot less. They have little concern as to the expenses of the union leaders as long as they get their union wages. They have little concern that older retired members of their union are receiving very little in pension, although if it were not for them they would not be receiving premium pay.

The philosophy of unions is appropriate and I am sure some of them are reputable, but the management of some of them has serious issues.

(101) Business partners

I would not suggest this, as it is a lot like lending money to relatives. The only reason I can think of to be a business partner is that the other partner has more to offer the success of the partnership than you do. Then after the fact, you think that you do.

(102) Big government

You can not discuss *big government* without discussing the Conservative group in this country as well as Socialism. The reason being that Conservative philosophy is defiant against big government. The problem with this is that what they are actually against is how much money the government spends. Of course the other aspect is that big government limits others profits due to regulations. I will leave the regulations limiting their profits, by saying that regulations protect the citizens from large businesses and corporations as well as protecting large businesses and corporations from each other. I have no idea how many of these regulations are necessary, but I suspect most of them, as they were argued by legislators before being enacted.

The U.S. is the most socialist society and the most capitalistic society in the world and has been for years. It also has the biggest government in the world. If someone gave you an island the size of the U.S., would you divide it up into 50 small states with their own governments and then divide these states into 30 or so smaller counties with their own governments and then add 100 cities in each county with their own governments? If you did, you would have to be a crazy person and you would end up with the most governed country in the world. The duplication of efforts is staggering and the least cost efficient system I could ever dream of. All of these many governments have social programs, regulations and laws that make it obvious that we are the most socialistic country in the world. In effect these governments are questionably governed (but not really) by a national government that distributes money to help finance their social programs. The private sector of course is regulated by federal, state, county and local regulations. So is the *federal government* to big, or is it a combination of the different regulations and the money spent and the employees of all of the different governments combined? Of course the citizenry pays taxes to all of them.

Due to our historical evolution, the U.S. government had no design or any choice but to end up with fifty states or it would not have. If there is a positive side to this situation, it is that these governments are probably the largest employers in the U.S. The governments spend the tax revenue and the employees pay taxes on their wages. Of course this is a net loss for the federal government and this is supplemented by private enterprise taxes and what we can borrow from the citizens and other governments. That is what they call a budget deficit.

This deficit can only be reduced by receiving taxes and reducing expenditures. There are few social expenditures by the U.S. government, which are not beneficial or necessary to some portion of the society. Realistic cuts would be to government subsidies to entities that do not now require them. The answer is not to increase taxes, but to increase the number of taxable incomes. If we doubled our work force, we would triple our federal revenue. I have addressed how to increase our taxable incomes and will not repeat it because anyone should be able to figure that out, but then again they don't seem to be able to. As this portion, mainly pertains to the Conservative philosophy, I will temper it with the inability of the Liberals (the workers friend) to be able to figure it out either. I really don't know what the philosophy of the Liberals is. It appears to be social programs for the citizenry which they can't pay for, and I think if they could pay for them the Conservatives would be satisfied with that as long as the private sector got their share. As far as the Democrat and Republican congressmen are concerned, the Congress is the biggest game in town and they love to play games and they went to great lengths to be an addition to big government.

Are all of the people in this country brain locked to bitching, arguing and obligated to someone else or some group to divert their attention to the fact that more jobs and more U.S. manufacturing is the solution to the problem, not reducing big government.

Just an afterthought, but the U.S. has revenue from other sources. I may be repeating myself when I ask why the residents of Alaska receive oil production revenues when we in the lower 48 bought Alaska with our money? I am also curious what Louisiana did with the billions and billions of dollars of oil revenue they received from the oil companies. It obviously was not used to upgrade the housing, building of dikes or for spilled oil recovery equipment. Their infrastructure has been explained to me as near non-existent. Where is the money, while the U.S. government spends millions on Louisiana?

(103)   Groups, individuals and philosophies who want to run the U.S. Government.

An ironic thing about trying to write a book about ones own perception of things is that it takes a lot of time and this being the case, I am receiving new information every day and any new information can have the effect of changing ones perception to some degree. Just recently I have been acquiring information which has done just that. I don't know if it changed my perception all that much, but it has changed it somewhat. What I am referring to is the realization of something I had really not given enough thought earlier. That being in respect to the matter or topic of the control of the U.S. Government.

There are people, groups, institutions and political parties who are saying one thing and actually meaning something else. They are saying that this is the greatest country in the world. Logic dictates that this statement refers to the U.S. government at this very moment. You never hear that this *could* be the greatest country in the world, or it is *almost* the greatest country in the world. Any statement by them is of course bias anyway because they are U.S. citizens. I am sure there are other people in other countries saying the same thing about their country.

I would even accept a statement that this is the greatest country in the world, but it could be better. In lieu of this we are deluged with what is wrong with this country today, being the fault of the current administration, as well as what was wrong with the U.S. under the previous administration. With all of these continuous faults, which include all of the reasons we are going to self-destruct, it gives the false impression that we are *not* the best country in the world. I am sure our enemies just love this kind of rhetoric as it saves them the trouble of manufacturing it. I suspect that we have a tremendous audience in the Middle East for news commentary shows such as FOX and MSNBC.

Actually what these people or groups who wants to save us from a previous administration believe, is that **the U.S. will be the greatest country in the world if they have control of the government** and make necessary changes. If they do not get control, the U.S. is somehow going to self-destruct due to incompetence, mismanagement, philosophical beliefs and so on. Only their philosophical beliefs can save us.

In their mind, they have the U.S. sitting on a pinnacle of righteousness with them at the helm and this righteousness is only possible with them at this helm.

I do not deny that the U.S. is the greatest country in the world, but it would be arrogant of me to picture the U.S. as a *super culture*, considering the poverty, social problems, our economy, our financial institutions, our infrastructure, unemployment and so on.

The people who contend that they are our only salvation are completely out of touch with reality, which for the most part is because they have never had to contend with reality or it has been so long that they have forgotten it. If they were dealing with some other people's reality, they could not be in a position to run this country by spending millions of dollars to get there.

Large groups and millions of people have been believing what these saviors have been preaching for the last 200 years and usually these saviors did not acquire the control of the government, and low and behold we are still here and we are still the best country in the world. To their distaste, this may simply be because these people were not able to gain control of the U.S. government.

I am not sure that the U.S. or the rest of civilization for that matter, will ever see another century due to divine intervention or international conflict, but I am certain that the U.S. will not self-destruct because a specific philosophical group did not gain power over the government.

Mistakes are made by the government, some large and some small, but even a totally polarized Congress or Whitehouse will not commit national suicide, or will it be allowed too.

The sad thing about this lust by groups to save the U.S. is that in reality, these groups want to run this country for their own self-interest and not the interest of every citizen of the U.S. I contend that for the most part, these groups actually believe that they are essential to the salvation of the U.S. and the citizens, but when they think of the citizens, they are thinking of the vast numbers who are similar to them and do not have a clue as to the vast number not similar to them. These people who are not similar are perceived as the source of all of the problems anyway.

When thinking of the Presidency, I have always thought or believed that regardless of the person, the job dictates what must be done. I think all new Presidents realize this in short order. A new President who would previously never kill a fly, within months may be destined to killing thousands of the enemy. They do the job regardless of any beliefs or preconceived ideas, because they have to.

To summarize this topic; Every four years the population is deluged with information of which a vast amount is not true, is propaganda and is extremely cynical and frightening. The thought is presented that this is our last chance to save the U.S. and to save the country from the hands of the current incompetent administrations.

What this actually does over time is to destroy the credibility of the U.S. government in the eyes of the people. Young people are indoctrinated as to the unscrupulous character of the U.S. Congress and most Presidents. This has had the effect, which you see in approval ratings of any segment of the U.S. Government. There is a national cynical attitude among all citizens and for the most part it is based on nothing more than propaganda from self-interest groups.

The only thing worse than originating such propaganda is unquestionably believing it. If the government makes a mistake, we should not exclusively condemn the government officials, we should condemn the groups and people who are responsible and took part, no matter how small a part, in getting all of these people elected. The damage was done before the mistake was made.

I apparently have an unpopular perception, it being the positive aspects of the U.S. Government in respect to governing this nation regardless of the party in control, and its resilience based upon The Constitution, The Bill of Rights and the character of *ALL* of the citizens of the U.S., not just select groups.

(104) The influence of movies on our society

My perception of this issue is that movies have definitely had a great influence on our society. This influence for the most part has been detrimental and is felt most by the younger people. It has been determined by the majority of Americans since our existence as a nation, that there are things that should not be witnessed or read by children and this continues to this day. There are some who do not agree with this philosophy. The people or groups who have a philosophy of proliferation of such material among children are those who can profit from it, those who have extreme religious beliefs, those who argue their philosophical beliefs from an extreme liberal point of view and some Constitutionalists.

There has never been a time that there were not laws or social taboos to protect children from sexual or violent content in books and movies. Children are aware of this and it enhances their curiosity and their devious level of interest. As is the case, there is a huge market out there, which are the children themselves. What a child sees cattle do on a cattle ranch has to be considered an acceptable experience and should be accompanied by a long explanation. Consciously including this scene in a fiction movie would not be acceptable.

Throughout the years, the movie industry has pushed the legal limits pertaining to sexual and violent content. This being the case, movie producers could never be certain that they could get away with it and it was an expensive risk. At some point, some bright individual developed the movie-rating scheme as a way to avoid the black and white of laws and public policy. We now have movies rated as to who can attend them based upon age and parental permission. We have, G, PG13, R and whatever ratings. This rating system relies on some individuals who rate these movies in coordination with the movie industry and puts the burden upon parental or adult guidance. Enforcement is by movie theater owners and the honor system. This rating system was under public scrutiny for a short time and apparently the public was satisfied with the results or they had no choice in the matter. Since that time the movie content has slowly evolved to the point that at least, I think it is not acceptable.

I may be somewhat of a prude when it comes to watching sexual or violent content in a crowd and I become very uncomfortable watching the sexual content available when there are children 13 and over sitting in front or next to me. Of course this is PG.13 and perfectly legitimate, but to me it is moral decadence imposed upon the thirteen year old. This content is not only portrayed as being socially acceptable, but it is portrayed as very desirable and pleasurable *and must be OK*, because we the citizens have as much as told them so by allowing it to be watched. They are watching a fiction world on screen and living in a nonfiction world in real life. The violence in movies is as disturbing; in that young people are getting a false reality in respect to the ability of the human body to endure damage and pain. On the screen it is common to see someone hit repeatedly with a steel pipe and miraculously in a matter of seconds, they recover from the blows and win the fight, which would have immobilized each of the fighters a dozen times. This false sense of indestructibility may be the direct cause of ridiculously dangerous tricks by teenagers. As well, it may also contribute to the mentality and violent nature of young gang members who appear to believe that they are indestructible.

Teenagers today are watching content that would make most adults blush in the past. Cable and satellite television is going down the same path and of course are showing R rated programs and movies where there is no parental supervision at all.

Young boys are less influenced by this content because they are all too familiar with every conceivable sexual encounter and just want to participate.

Young girls are not so lucky. The content of movies, TV and books paint a fantasy picture of a society and personal relationships which is a far cry from reality and they are buying into it. For this reason, when their life experiences are not typical of the fantasy world, they are dissatisfied and think they are not in the right social group or have the wrong partner. This has a very detrimental effect upon any personal relationships they have during their lives. There are those, regardless of movies, who see the light and the reality of life pretty quickly and have to adapt to it, and these are the lucky ones.

(105) Unmarried partners and premarital sex

More common than not, and now socially acceptable (except by most fathers and mothers) is the practice of a young male and female living together without being married. My perception of this situation is that *I don't care*. It may be Ok and it may not be Ok, but whatever the result, it is going to be their problem. It is just two people thinking they know what is appropriate for them. Sometimes it works and sometimes it doesn't. My experience from afar is that it usually doesn't. I attribute this to marriages as well.

I do question why a male and a female live together without getting married. The obvious answer is that one or both of them do not want to be obligated for life and one or both of them are not worried about losing their partner due to a somewhat loose relationship.

The whole scenario seems a little tumultuous to me, and then, *OOOPS*; there is a child on the way. The situation started out as a recipe for disaster and now we have one in the oven. This is where the actions of two people will result in problems that will affect many others. Sometimes this event is a blessing and sometimes it is decades of involvement of grandparents, social institutions and the courts. Someone has to raise and care for the child for eighteen years at the cost of $100,000.00. Who is it going to be?

(106) Pure capitalism and socialism

Pure capitalism and pure socialism as a country's governmental policies and endeavors, have proven beyond any doubt that they do not work and in fact can not exist for any period of time. As we are neither, we have managed to hang in there to this point. The danger is that we may not continue to function as a country with both socialistic and capitalistic policies. As politics actually determines our future in respect to capitalism and socialism, it is possible that this country could be directed one way or the other. The closer we get to pure socialism or pure capitalism the closer we are to our own demise.

Capitalists in this country think that we are a capitalistic country and they are beating the drums to further their capitalistic ideology. Socialists in this country think we are what we actually are. The reason socialists do not believe that this should be a pure socialistic country is because they have eyes and they also realize that capitalism is the engine driving the benefits of social policies. Capitalists believe that the country can sustain itself as a pure capitalistic country. That is far from true, because capitalism has little respect for the working class and no respect for any who are not working. In reality, pure capitalism breeds a social undercurrent, which will eventually demand pure socialism as a backlash solution. Capitalism controls the wealth in this country and as can be seen in other countries in the past and recently, when a situation arises where the wealthy control a country and the working class is financially stressed, a major problem arises. When this happens the capitalists are absolutely shocked as they had no idea of the repercussions. They are taken by complete surprise.

Until the time of crisis, the socialists will be demanding more of the capitalist, as that is where the money is. As things get worse, there will be a movement to share the wealth, which will not set well with the capitalists as it is their wealth and they worked for it. In our country with a Congress and a President which all can be either aligned with socialists or capitalists, all legislation could be preferentially direct to one ideology or the other. This scenario could not sustain itself for very long. It is in fact in the hands of the voters in this country. When push comes to shove and reality sits in and the votes are counted, I suspect there will be more people voting for social programs than for capitalistic ideals. There will be a sharing of the wealth by way of taxation and social programs. Now this will not be good news for capitalists who instigated their own situation.

Capitalists are no friend to Socialists and Socialists are no friend to Capitalists and there is no compassion between them. Money and power drives capitalists and I defy you to find one who does not like both or they would not be capitalists. That is what capitalism is. Whereas present socialistic ideals in the U.S. are based on mutual benefits to all with an industrial and financial system based upon social equality, but not necessarily financial equality.

As this is somewhat of an oil and water mixture, the problems are obvious. The obvious solution to the problem is to not push the other faction off the cliff. Maintain a social structure where the least wealthy can reasonably survive and can better themselves financially depending on their effort. Create jobs so that we will have more consumers paying more taxes and purchasing more from the wealthy capitalists. Make a climate available to the private sector whereby it is beneficial for them to reinvest in industry. I have explained my thoughts on turning the economy around earlier in this book.

The bottom line is that we must ignore extremists and egomaniacs whose motives are just self-satisfying.

These people perceive this whole thing as a game, and it is not a game. They will realize it is not a game when people of good sense displace them. Use all of the good qualities of capitalism and the good qualities of socialism, as on their own, one is no better than the other and on their own they will not work. Our problems are initiated from the far left and the far right and their philosophies are not compatible with a stable government or life, liberty, and the pursuit of happiness.

(107) Assholes (2011)

Everyone knows what an asshole is because during their life they have come in contact with them, as they are a good portion of our society.

My perception of an asshole is generally someone of some degree of authority over others or considers himself more intelligent or just may be more wealthy. Having this position, they are inconsiderate as to other people's thoughts or wellbeing and mentally abuse those over which they express their feeling of superiority. To me this brings to mind Rush Limbaugh and Donald Trump, who without question are both assholes. There are millions of others as you well know, you have met them. A lot of these can be excused because they are hired to be assholes and it goes with the job and the money. As for Rush and Donald, they are true assholes because they love being assholes. Arrogance, lack of humility and the love of abuse to inferiors (which is everybody else) is what they enjoy. Assholes can be generally depicted as bullies. Why people like or put up with bullies, I don't know.

(108) Medical doctors

Why anyone would want to be a doctor is a mystery to me. Thank God there are many that do. It can't possibly be the money. Those I know work ridiculous long hours and have a distasteful job. I excuse them for their choice of occupation because they are much more intelligent than I, and I am sure they have made the right decision because of this. If they are doing it for the betterment of us patients, God bless them.

Not making too much of the issue, you dentists and optometrists are doing it for the money. No disrespect meant, because they undertook the effort to further their education so that you would have a good paying job.

(109) Sin tax

The self-righteous people in the U.S. are the first to advocate sin taxes. Of course righteous means that they do not partake of that particular product which is considered sinful. Usually sin taxes are on alcoholic beverages and tobacco products. To the wealthy, this is of no consequence because these taxes are insignificant due to their wealth.

Alcohol is an addictive product as well as used for social purposes. Tobacco products are just addictive, now that the social aspects of them have been lost. In either case, in the short term and the long term, both products have a financial effect upon the user's family. To my knowledge, taxes on these products have only contributed to very few nicotine addicts stopping the use of tobacco products and probably no alcoholics quitting drinking.

This was not the case in my family, but those of us familiar with the financial hardships to a family due to having an alcoholic parent understand the plight of the family members. A terrible situation is made even worse by a sin tax on alcohol. This tax is paid at the expense of the alcoholic's family. This can also be said for $7.00 a pack cigarettes. Sin tax is a user's tax, but the family of the user is paying it.

Beyond being punished by the righteous for using these products, there is definitely a good aspect of these taxes and some well-meaning people gave this consideration when establishing the tax. Tobacco products are now cost prohibitive for most young people and it definitely has reduced the number of smokers in the U.S.

Due to my experience and the above knowledge I have, my perception of an appropriate tax on these products would be one where the older people pay considerably less tax than the new user. Everything else is grandfathered, why not the sin tax? I understand the problem of an older person buying these products for the young people. (That rings a bell with me) We just have older people sign in the grocer's book that they are buying the product for personal consumption and if they get caught doing otherwise, they are in deep trouble, like tax fraud. That ought to do it.

The families of users of these products should not have to suffer due to these excessive taxes.

(110) Inheritance or death taxes

I do not understand the concept of such taxes. In my case, inheritance taxes must be good for me as I won't be paying any and the wealthy will pay taxes from which I benefit.

Because it will be beneficial to me does not make it right. That is kind of an un-American position, but it is true. One of the problems with this tax even if is justified, is that there are a thousand different ways to circumvent the tax to some degree. We have scores of attorneys and tax accountants doing just this. Multitudes of hours have also been spent by Congress adopting legislation creating these loopholes.

I do understand that great wealth almost always increases over time and there will eventually be a super wealthy class, which is of little benefit to the U.S. If you have more money than you can spend, you just don't spend it.

I may be wrong, but I believe the inheritance tax is just a revenue tool by governments and has little to do with prohibiting acquired excess wealth.

(111) Why do politicians and political hopefuls do stupid things?

As for the politicians who do stupid things. I perceive stupid things as actions like getting videotaped accepting bribes, making inappropriate deals with business interests, getting in a drunken brawl in a bar, frequenting houses of ill repute, having illicit affairs, etc. The risk factor of these actions is extremely high and is downright reckless. My perception of why they do these things is that for years they have been surrounded by dozens of other politicians that have done the same thing. Those were the good old days, Congressman. Now we have mini-mini cameras, people suing at the drop of a hat or more than eager to sign a million-dollar book deal explaining the Congressman's involvement.

Another aspect is that for some reason they think they can just lie and everything will go away. In our current atmosphere of cutthroat politics where every word is analyzed, lies are readily accepted by ones peers, but don't work all that well on national TV.

Now as for political hopefuls, and in their defense, most of their past discretions and stupid statements were made before they entered or understood politics. Not all though, there are many vying for public office and still making stupid statements. The problem with these people is that they don't know they are making stupid statements and are just showing their ignorance. Being bright is not a prerequisite for being elected anyway. The prerequisite is getting people to vote for you regardless of what you say.

(112) Hate mail

This is what I call the political emails I get. By design, there are hundreds of millions of these hate emails sent every day. In the world of politics we no longer have opponents.

We have, scum suckers, idiots, traitors, anti-American and so on with accompanying jokes and cartoons of totally inappropriate, degrading or malicious content. We don't just disagree with opponents who are now dire enemies; we hate them and all they stand for.

These emails as perceived by me are absolutely inappropriate behavior. On top of that, it is easily proven that 90% of these emails are false information or downright lies.

By the content and the technical layout and design of these emails, it is easy to determine that they were produced at great effort and expense by individuals or groups unknown. They are never a simple email as sent between individuals. Taken as a whole, I consider these emails as part of a conspiracy to eliminate certain individuals or parties from public office. These are essentially negative advertisements, usually false, in lieu of the attributes of their own candidate or party. As for me, I would never vote for a candidate who is involved in such hate mail practice, or if most of his followers do.

If our Middle Eastern enemies receive these American emails, no wonder they can justify hating us, we hate each other, and confirm that our government and politicians are scum-sucking rats of no moral character. Hey, that's a good idea for a business. I could sell Al Qaida my hate mail and they would probably pay a fortune for it, and I am getting it free.

To finish this topic, I have past acquaintances that used to be involved in politics in a reasonable manner, and today they are fanatics to the point I am concerned about the effect it is having on them.

I have read and heard so much of this trash that I am concerned about the effect it is having *on me.*

(113) The new telephones

We now have 3G, 4G, and every possible concept that can be utilized on a small hand held device. It appears that a person could be stranded alone on a deserted island and live a fairly normal life if he had one of these. I assume by now that they have small solar panels for charging.

For those that have these devices and do not live on a deserted island, a good portion of the population wishes they did. More *big government.* Now we have to have laws that say you can't use one of these visually demanding devices while you are driving down the highway at seventy miles per hour. If not avoiding a collision, *usually with a young lady with a phone to her ear who looks at your car and never even sees it*, the general public is persistently startled or distracted by every conceivable noise, which they call ring tones.

I swear there are people who walk around every awake moment with one of these in their hand. The amazing thing is the frequency that these people communicate on these. I am sure it can be measured in minutes between calls or texts. I have a cell phone and it very rarely rings and I rarely make a call on it. Maybe I don't have any friends or maybe they are old fogies like me. Who is making all of these calls and what the hell could they persistently be talking about.

Then there is texting, which I don't even want to go into because it makes no sense if you have a telephone in your hand.

I will admit to being very hypocritical on this issue, as I go overboard on a lot of electronic and video equipment, but then again it is my perception of these phones and you can compare your perception against mine. I will also admit that if I had one of these *phones,* I would probably change my perception of them.

(114) Simple mindedness

Being simple-minded, as I perceive of it and define it, has for the most part little to do with a person's intelligence. A simple-minded person is just a person who thinks that every task or problem has a simple solution. Now whatever the opposite of simple-minded is describes me. No task, subject or object is a simple matter for me. For years I have heard comments like, **just** *(I hate this word)*, and other words or phrases which imply that a complex issue is really very easy to solve. It's easy; *just* raise taxes, *just* cut taxes, *just* cut government spending, *just* cut subsidies, *just* veto it, *just* read the directions, *just* don't do anything, and so on.

I hear these comments and think of all of the repercussions of this less than intellectual advice. Being simple-minded is when you think you can just easily solve the issue without giving any thought as to all of the repercussions. I may be perceived as a person who over thinks things, which is obviously the case, but under thinking issues has screwed us nearly to death in this country, and it is happening right now. The *just* people out there do not have a clue as to the complexity of issues such as; our financial system, international diplomacy, social programs, illegal aliens, recession, international finance, industry, the extreme poor and wealthy, selection of potential political candidates, and so on. If they did, at least we would all have similar information to have considered and discussions would be more rational.

(115) Reality shows

A reality show is two teams of ten people each, dressed in rags, sitting in the blazing sun, worrying about whether or not they are going to die of thirst or hunger. If it was me, I would strangle the three cameramen and their sound crews and steal all of the water and food from their motor homes down the beach out of sight.

I do watch the Pawn Broker show, which is an **unreality show.** There never has been a pawnbroker with the morality shown in this program. That's not what pawnbrokers do.

Excluding the Antique Road Show and The Deadliest Catch, they all have issues and I wonder if everybody else watches them thinking the same thing I do. "What a joke."

(116) Blood is thicker than water

Is blood thicker than water? Of course this phrase is pertaining to what we call blood relative, being that they have a close genetic link to us.

The simple answer to this question is, No. I only need to give one example to prove this, but I will furnish you with two. The first being your loving spouse and the second being adopted children. The only distasteful scenario to prove this is in a dire situation where you are limited to the people you can save. Your spouse, which is not genetically linked to you in any way and your adopted child, if you only have one child to save, will be your first selections over any blood relatives.

(117) Sleep

I wonder about sleep. Why do I have different sleeping habits then most people? Most people go to sleep in the evening and wake early in the morning. I go to bed at 2:00 am and get up between 7:30 and 9:00 am. Most people get seven to nine hours sleep a night and I get five and a half to seven hours sleep. A lot of people take naps during the day and I rarely do. Do I require less sleep or do I drive myself to stay awake when I should be sleeping. I asked my doctor and he said that he only sleeps five hours per night. I don't even have a perception as to this problem, but I have a guess. My guess is that the normal human body would like eight hours sleep per night. People who sleep less do it by choice, usually to take advantage of consciousness. I have a lot of things to do at night when uninterrupted. When I do go to bed I am really tired. People like me are probably in some way doing physical or psychological damage to their body, I don't know. On the other hand there are people who may be sleeping too much and in fact they enjoy it, whereas I do not.

There is a possibility that among the reasons for sleep, one of the major factors could be the psychological need to stop and start rather than an uninterrupted ongoing consciousness. The brain may be needing the break, more so than the body.

(118) Equipment maintenance

Now this may be a peculiar topic, but is of more concern to some than people think. Equipment maintenance is where you keep equipment in as close to new condition as you can. I perceive that there are two schools of thought on this matter. The first being **over** maintenance and the second being **under** maintenance.

Being an under maintenance person, I quickly see the problems with over maintenance. Over maintenance is usually associated with equipment that is not required to do heavy work every single day. The cost and time involved doing maintenance in the working world is not cost effective and there is argument that it should be put off until the equipment breaks or it is not being used. If it breaks, you have an optional piece of equipment to take its place or patch it together until the job is finished. For the daylight until dark farming, logging, construction world, this is normally the case. Of course they are prepared to fix the equipment when it breaks. Equipment is breaking down in the field all of the time, which would not be the case if you fixed every leak and squeak at an expense of money and time. Of course oil changes and so on take place not as a matter of physical maintenance.

Maintenance on your big four-wheel drive diesel pickup is another matter and is quite expensive. They were not built to be easily repaired, particularly by the owner, so he performs over maintenance at great expense on things, which may have lasted, long after he traded it in.

In reality you cannot over maintain a piece of equipment if you have the time and want to spend the money. Heavy users of industrial equipment don't have the time and do not care to gamble with the money that a piece of equipment is going to break before the job is finished. They have welders, torches, parts, and don't fix it until it breaks or just sit it aside. They don't try to keep it in like new condition; they keep it in workable condition.

(119) Amazed at the value of things

The value of things as perceived by people always amazes me. For the typical sportsman gun owner, their mind cannot get around the fact that their pristine Model 270 rifle, in the wool case, is of the same value as a beat up old junker car. This doesn't even equate. The value of their 270 in their mind is always compared to other guns, not junker cars.

This scenario of the value of things is pretty much the same in respect to everything in that mentally it doesn't make sense. Have you noticed that if you own it, it isn't worth anything, but if you want another one it will cost you an arm and a leg? This is quite common in respect to antiques around your house, if you have any. They are 150 years old and they are worth two dollars. Whatever you have nobody seems to want and what you want is always very expensive. Well, one man's treasured item is perceived as junk by the next guy. Of course this is not always the case and that is what keeps pawnshops and antique stores in business. Of course the big winner is Goodwill.

(120) Petroleum products and their effects on America

This subject brings to mind a Saber Tooth Tiger who jumps on a camel that just seems to be standing knee deep in water and doesn't even move when the tiger approaches. It looked like an easy meal, but suddenly the tiger notices that he cannot move his legs and the more he fights to get free, the more he sinks into the Berkley Tar Pit.

This scenario took place thousands of years ago, but is strikingly similar to where we are today. We can appreciate the tiger's frustration of not being able to break free of the petroleum bondage and we continue to mass-produce equipment dependent on more and more petroleum and we are sinking just as the tiger did. Humans did not discover oil, the camel and the tiger did. Oil has been lying around for thousands of years, but there just wasn't any use for it.

As soon as there was a use for it by American citizens, there was the boom and bust scenario. During the boom, Standard Oil and others made their fortunes. The bust came when it was realized that there was so much available oil in Pennsylvania, Oklahoma, Texas, California and other locations that you could hardly give it away. Oil and petroleum products were dirt cheap to consumers and that was the beginning of Americans becoming spoiled in respect to petroleum product prices. The rest of the international industrialized nations had more respect for the benefits of oil to a society, primarily because they did not have any oil resources of their own. As demand increased dramatically in the U.S. and the consumption was such that a few oil companies, I assume by design, quickly figured out that they could actually control the petroleum industry and oil supply all around the world. Cheap oil and gasoline meant the mass production of petroleum using devices. Cheap oil to the consumers was a marketing tool to insure a vast future in petroleum sales. To facilitate the newly required volumes of cheap oil worldwide, the oil companies went to where there was the most abundant cheap oil available. This was the Middle East. Middle East countries for the most part were still inhabited by citizens riding camels and had Sheiks, tribal leaders and the like.

Arrangements were made by large oil companies to stabilize these governments and this stabilization process took many forms. Whatever was necessary to obtain a secure source of oil from a country, these arrangements were made. Hence, the world continued to receive cheap oil.

A lot has changed since then although the major oil companies still maintain their control over the production of oil and have a considerable amount to do with the price of oil. I mention earlier in this book a spicket where the oil supply can be turned off or regulated. At present we have two spickets. The first being at the source country and the second being at the major oil companies producing or distributing petroleum products. The third party involved in this unseemly crowd is the commodity and futures market. These big three determine the price of oil and what we pay for petroleum products.

The oil companies have determined that the marketing tool of supplying cheap oil to increase the numbers of vehicles, aircraft, boats, and so on is at the point that it is no longer required. We fell into the tar pit trap of immediately manufacturing very inefficient petroleum consuming devices due to the cheap supply of fuel. If not for cheap petroleum for decades, we would right now all be driving smaller more fuel efficient vehicles and be happier than larks because we would not know any better. Of course gasoline would then be $8.00 a gallon. (Get the picture?) We consumers have no control over the price of oil other than to quit using it altogether. That not being possible, we are screwed by oil source countries, oil companies and those manipulating prices on Wall Street. Countries hold a threat over our head, oil companies are basically thumbing their noses at us and multimillions are made daily on Wall Street.

I worked in the Prudhoe Bay oil fields in Alaska and distinctly recall seeing a daily graph of the current oil prices. What I saw was oil selling for $12.00 per barrel. There had been some layoffs and the word was that they could make money at $12.00 per barrel, but that was about as low as it could go. They were pumping oil at $12.00 per barrel and making a profit. Let's say for the sake of this book that they must have been making $6.00 per barrel profit to make it worthwhile. When oil hit $18.00 per barrel, they must have doubled their profit margin or $12.00 per barrel. When oil hit $114.00 per barrel, their profit went from $6.00 per barrel to $108.00 per barrel. In all fairness, there may have been more expenses, so let's just knock it down to $50.00 per barrel profit.

Can you even comprehend the amount of money being made? The same situation took place in all of the oil producing countries during the same period.

This has been my perception of the *Cause* of our petroleum problems and now I would like to give you my perception of the *Effects* of it.

Every American and every aspect of American life is affected by the current high price of petroleum products. For a few this is a positive effect, for some it makes little difference, but for the vast majority of Americans it has a very negative effect on their life. The instances of where this occurs are so vast that a listing would be near impossible.

The obvious instance is the price of gasoline and diesel at the pump. What happened when fuel went from $2.25 per gallon to a high of around $4.00? For a starter, everything for sale that consumed large quantities of fuel was not marketable at even a small loss. Similar privately owned equipment was parked. For every commodity worldwide which required being harvested, manufactured, hauled, or in any way consumed fuel, there was a surcharge added to the consumer price and it was passed on to the consumer. Now you fill up your gas tank for $75.00 and pay at least 25% more for everything you purchase. I am not going to attribute all of this to the price of fuel, but check the price of a McDonalds hamburger or the prices at Wendy's and Arby's as compared to just a few years ago. There is enough evidence to show that the price of labor has not driven these prices up, so what is it? Even the increase in fuel prices does not justify these higher prices. Is it that everyone has less to spend due to fuel prices and *low and behold* the prices have gone up on consumables to maintain the profit margin because there are fewer customers?

This problem has fueled the Green Revolution, which is probably a good thing, but was not introduced in a timely or well-planned manner. We are jumping into reflex mode to try to solve our petroleum based energy requirements when we should have started this fifty years earlier, not yesterday. We have a real mess on our hands, speaking as one of the majority of Americans whose lifestyle has been interrupted by the price of petroleum products. Granted that to the wealthy, these price increases are insignificant to their budgets. The private sector just passes on their increased production costs to consumers who must pay them. All of this relates to the price of petroleum products and it is squeezing the life out of the middle and lower class wage earners in this country. The increase cost of getting to their place of employment equates to a cut in wages at a time of flat wages. The loss of finances a family has to spend has increased dramatically due to the price of fuel and therefore the average American's standard of living has decreased. This whole scenario can be compared to a tax increase to the consumer, but instead of the tax going to the Government, it is going to oil producing countries and oil companies. If gasoline had stayed at $2.25 per gallon, which was still making them rich, and the U.S. Government had put on a

$1.75 per gallon sales tax, what do you think our annual deficit would be?

We are afraid of oil producing countries and we are afraid of oil companies. They have us by the ----- and our Government knows it.

Defying any kind of logic, there are individuals who have legislative power in this country who are adamant about subsidizing oil companies, giving them tax cuts and legislating tax loopholes for them to utilize. Trying to justify such a position, I have concluded that these people have or will be enriching themselves politically, financially in the present or future or have a family member being held hostage under threat of bodily harm. The first two options are reprehensible, although just good business practice, and in the case of the third option, Congressman, I would do the same thing.

As you don't have to be very smart to figure out what is wrong with something, you do in order to solve the problem in a reasonable manner. Not being one who is overly smart, all I can do is just comment on the matter, and like or unlike other people, mull over the possibilities rather than solve them.

My perception, in random thoughts, as to potential solutions to the problem is as follows:

In the event of a dire national crisis we could nationalize all of the oil companies inside of our counties territory. A crisis such as this would be when oil producing countries would not ship oil to the U.S. and oil companies in our territory would refuse to meet our demands as to all production going to the U.S. This would include their refusal to drill at 100% capacity or refuse to do anything the U.S. demanded to save our country.

When just the price of oil is the issue and it is eventually decided by our entire Government that the U.S. can no longer survive under the thumb of the oil producers, we have no choice but to reduce consumption drastically and that being oil from foreign sources. That being the case, and desiring to sustain our lifestyle, we have to get the equivalent of that reduction from alternate energy sources. This would require drilling for oil and developing located oil sources. This would do us little good if it was done by present oil companies, because the price of gasoline now is due to oil company profits. The U.S. Government was able to start from nothing and construct the Manhattan Project, Grand Coulee Dam, Hoover Dam and dozens of others. We could build a highway through the wilderness to Alaska and put a man on the Moon, so don't tell me we are totally dependent on the technology that oil companies have. Even if that were the case, I perceive that thousands would jump ship for such a project as maximized oil production in the U.S. We can develop the oil shale and other types of oil deposits and we can use more natural gas and coal. We can throw up 100,000 wind turbines and photoelectric panels by the square mile.

We can totally eliminate our consumption of foreign oil, so why haven't we?

Well, we have too many people and a great deal of them in political positions who are perfectly satisfied where we are. They are content to live the good life at the expense of others and perceive themselves as being on the winning side of this issue without a clue of the consequences because they do not live in a world of consequences. One day they are going to wake up to a news flash and be absolutely shocked at what has just happened. It wasn't supposed to work this way. It has happened time and time again to this country.   Pearl Harbor and 9/11 to mention a couple.

No oil from foreign countries would make these pale in comparison.

On the path we are taking we will see $10.00 per gallon gasoline and we had better plan on it now. We have people who will go to any lengths to go back to the good old days and people for who these are the good old days and want to maintain a status quo. I perceive that we can never go back to the good old days, the present good old days will pass and we have to at least try for the good new days. These good new days are entirely possible, but it takes progressive thought processes, not regressive.

The Founders of the Constitution and the Bill of Rights were thinking of the good new days, realizing that our society and country was not static and could not persevere counting on the actions of other countries, other philosophies or individuals, no matter how highly placed.

(121) Deficit spending

My perception of deficit spending is spending money you don't have. I don't think this is news to anybody else on this world.   The real question about deficit spending is whether it is acceptable or not.   Anyone who says it is not acceptable without further explanation is definitely a hypocrite. I don't believe that there is an individual in the U.S. who has not participated in deficit spending by choice. How many people out there have paid cash for everything they have ever bought or invested in?   This may have happened in the case of the extreme poor or the extreme rich, but rarely.   The terminology implies that you are spending money you do not have whether or not you eventually pay the expenditure. Deficit spending has become absolutely necessary for local, state and the federal government. It is really the only way you can absolutely pay for goods and services in a smooth orderly manner without having excess taxation. Very large construction projects would be nearly impossible without deficit spending.

Now the thing about deficit spending is that in order to maintain your ability to do so, you must show you have the ability to pay back borrowed money. This could be by putting up collateral, like your house or car, which is usually the case for average citizens. In the case of the U.S. Government the collateral is usually treasury bonds. We as citizens of a Democratic/Constitutional Republic have given our representatives the right to borrow money in our name as they see fit. Because the U.S. government has usually, and is spending more than it receives in revenue, the government borrows money from whatever source it can. A good deal of the time it is from the U.S. citizens.

Why do we spend more than we receive in revenue? We do this to maintain a level of life style and protect the U.S. from potential enemies, as well as protect U.S. citizens from each other. This being the case, we have what is called the National Debt and the title alone indicates that everyone in the nation owes this debt. We have a Democracy whereby we play ping pong in the government being run by two political parties who add to the debt and blame the other party. As for myself, I can equally give both parties the blame for the increase in the national debt, or the possibility is more likely that we should blame neither party.

What is obvious to everyone is that in order to reduce the national debt, we have choices. We can reduce government spending, raise taxes, raise revenue, or any combination of the three.

This is where we are confronted with the Liberal and Conservative philosophies or beliefs. And for the most part that is just what they are. They are not necessarily based on anything but personal beliefs and rational just gets in the way. Congress in session appears little different than a major league football game. You have the two teams on the field with the crowd cheering and you have the Conservative fans on one side of the field and the Liberals on the other. And you all know how Americans love football. Yelling and cheering for their respective teams and cussing at the fans on the other side.

Well, it shouldn't be a game, but as it is, the object of the game is to eliminate the deficit by acquiring money from one of the three choices they have.

My perception of the choices and options is somewhat different from others and it is the perception I have developed by the information I have come in contact with. Now I must admit that some of my sources of information come via television networks and I probably watch FOX news more than MSNBC. I watch FOX news out of curiosity of what is going to be said next, and MSNBC for the entertainment value. They are fair and balanced if you watch one an hour and then the other an hour and mentally combine them and drop the **fair** portion.

Back to choices. The U.S. government has an obligation to the citizens of the U.S. to make these choices.

Government spending.

In reality, cutting domestic government spending is cutting the cash flow to the U.S. economy. It is a reverse stimulus package. Not only that, the cut in cash flow compounds itself because the people who were receiving this money will now not only not have it to spend, they will not spend what they have been spending. Cutting this choice will be detrimental to the people included in the other two choices.

If we are just talking social services such as Medicare, Medicaid and Social Security, the same applies to some degree, but if they are cut to any significance, the ramifications of this have not even been imagined as yet. There is a major portion of the citizenry of the U.S. who is absolutely dependent on these services and cuts to them would be devastating as well as millions of family members of these people. Social unrest and its repercussions had better be given very serious consideration.

There is a distinct difference in cutting these social benefits for people who have millions of dollars in the bank and the people who would be devastated.

If these benefits are cut, they should be based on the need for these benefits. There are many millions of people who would graciously reduce their unnecessary benefits to assure those that require them receive them. And there are many millions who would not.

Raising taxes.

The primary roadblock to raising taxes is a philosophy that voting for raising taxes is equivalent to voting to go to Hell.

My perception of the raising taxes choice is taking into consideration what would happen if you raised taxes. It has been a fact forever that the best way to make money is not to get a lot from a few, but to get a little from many. Most of our capitalist system works on this principle.

What we must recognize is that the existing tax structure is defective and obsolete. People paying taxes have had over fifty years to determine how to lessen or eliminate their tax obligations. In every case it has been to the detriment of the U.S.

I paid $0.00 income tax last year and a corporation that had nine billion dollars profit paid $0.00 tax last year. Who in the hell is paying taxes? If you raised both of our taxes 10% we would both still pay $0.00 taxes.

On an individual basis I have heard many interviews of people of wealth who have clearly stated that they are in a high income category and have no problem with paying more taxes. I am sure low income individuals would pay some tax as they are recipients of social programs. Middle income people who receive W2 forms are already paying proportionally more than anyone else on their gross income, but I bet they would contribute a little to save America.

So if on an individual citizen basis, who is it that is yelling (absolutely no increase in taxes?) Other than Rush Limbaugh and the like, no one I am aware of. All I hear are people who seem to be saying, no new taxes on somebody else. These being the rich, the top 2%, small businesses, oil companies, etc.

I have negative thoughts about anyone having to pay 39% of their income in taxes. I don't think anyone should, but by the same token, I don't think anyone is. Show me a corporation that had a net profit of $100,000,000 before a multitude of deductions and paid $39,000,000 in taxes. Doesn't happen. What about the deductions? Well, you add up the deductions and other tax loopholes and 39% is a myth. What is a fair share? Hell, I don't know. Is graduated income tax fair? I don't think so. Is a flat rate

10% with no deductions more fair? Probably closer to being fair.

I can see no problem with raising taxes and no problem with a change in social benefits. Of course that is just me and I have no philosophical brain locked beliefs to contend with.

Raise revenue

The third choice I entertained was to raise revenue (not taxes.) My perception of how to raise revenue is merely to increase production. We should all buy U.S. goods and utilize our own natural resources. All of this I explained earlier in this book.

The third choice is the logical best choice and eliminates the need for the other two hard choices. In particular the first pertaining to social services which will be the most troublesome.

There are some who do not want any resolution to this country's problems because they thrive on them. If there isn't a problem they will create one. They psychologically require someone to hate. There are also those who are not content to just do their jobs as legislators. It is too mundane, not at all profitable and there are *powers that be* that you can rub shoulders with and entertain an intriguing life style while doing so.

(122) A nation of laws

When you hear this terminology it is almost always used in reference to a highly placed government official, who has committed a crime, and will, or will not be punished for it. In the reference you will also hear that he or his position is not above the law.

Normally the last thing a President does while in office is pardon the people who are not above the law. This is at the discretion of the President and the choices which are made as to pardons are sometimes very controversial. Pardons for non-violent crimes committed by members of the Presidents administration are all too common even though the laws broken have had a detrimental effect on the integrity of our government.

It is so common that individuals holding public office as high as the Vice President will not even be tried for these violations of the law because they are certain to be pardoned after an embarrassing trial.

In reality there is no one above the law in the U.S., but by the same token, there can be illegal acts performed by highly placed people and there will consequently be no penalty for the crime other than some public opinion. In the last few decades there have been very highly placed people who by law should have gone to prison for their offense. This did not happen and has made somewhat of a mockery of our justice system.

The point being, that these individuals have multitudes of lawyers for legal advice before committing these crimes, so they must have been aware that they were committing a crime at the time. This being the case, there was very good chance that they would be caught and it is inconceivable to me that they would have committed the crime without prior knowledge that they would be pardoned if caught. If this is true, the President may have been aware of the impending crime and was complicit in it.

Some of these offenses are lying before congressional hearings, which in affect is lying to every individual in the U.S. As lying under oath is rarely prosecuted in any court in the U.S., it is as well not pursued at congressional hearings. In every court room in the U.S., on a daily basis the defendant lies; or in divorce court and civil suits, both parties lie. Perjury is almost never prosecuted and for the most part is not even mentioned at the proceedings.

The judicial system in this country has given way too much authority to the presiding judge. When in court for the most minor of offenses such as a traffic ticket, the defendant is at the mercy of the judge in respect to being verbally abused or insulted. It seems an argument on your own behalf is completely out of order and borders on Contempt of Court. You may even be told to sit down and shut up. You can get off for court costs or the maximum penalty deciding upon how the judge is feeling that day or how much you pissed him off by thinking you had a right to speak. I have had limited experience in court, but what I have had has made a believer out of me. There are judges who should never be judges. Judge Judy is not unlike a great deal of them.

This is a bully's paradise.

As I seem to be covering all of the bases here, how about the attorneys? I have concluded that the average attorney is not going to piss the judge off on your behalf because he is going to have to deal with this judge on a daily basis. If the judge takes a disliking to a local attorney, he might as well move out of the area because every case he has before that judge will be influences to some degree. I will agree that there are probably thousands of very good judges in the U.S., but not all of them.

As for the laws currently on the books, which must include regulations and codes as all are enforced with a penalty, there are two perceptions.

The first perception is that there are many things we citizens can do and a few that are in violation of the law.

The second is that there are just a few things we can do and many that are in violation of the law.

I am compelled to go with perception number two. Just take a while and look around you no matter where you are and think of the laws that you could break near that location. Let's assume you are standing in the street in front of your house, which is against the law. You look at your property and start your list. I could only guess that there are at least a hundred different specific code and municipal requirements in respect to your property alone. There are too many to list here, but everything on or about your property is in compliance with a law, code or regulation. Then get in your car which is in the same situation and think about all of the laws pertaining to it. Drive down the street with your seat belt on and think of the multitudes of traffic laws and what you can't do with that car.

There are laws that pertain to everything that you and every other citizen in the U.S. do. I will just mention a small example of hundreds and that example is the fishing regulations for the State of Washington. I don't want to say over 1000 specific regulations, but I will. It is absolutely mind boggling. This is just one instance of regulations and laws which involve a very small part of human endeavors and there are hundreds of other human endeavors. The fishing regulations are like all other documents in respect to current law. You read them to determine what you can do, not what you can't.

My perception of this vast proliferation of laws is that we have these laws because we have to have them. Without them, there would be nothing but chaos. It is the curse of society that we must have these laws to protect us from each other as well as protect us from ourselves. Like everyone else, I violate a few of these now and then when I am confident I can get away with it.

The ironic thing is, we citizens of the U.S. are responsible for knowing these tens of thousands of laws. That is incomprehensible, but just go before a judge and tell him that you did not know you were breaking the law, and see where that gets you.

Yes I know, most of these laws change every year or so. Good luck.

(123) Intellectual curiosity

If I have not addressed this before, and if I did, time passes and thoughts change with time.

Throughout my life I have always been amazed at the lack of intellectual curiosity of most people. But, I will admit that there is intellectual curiosity and then there is intellectual curiosity. You have people that have to know how everything works and you have people that only care about how things that work that affect them personally. And then you have the majority of the people that don't care how anything works. It works or it doesn't and if it doesn't there is someone who does care how it works to fix it.

Most if not nearly all people can travel around the United States and see mountains, lakes, waterfalls, deserts, pine trees, sagebrush, valleys, rocks and everything else one would see. Rarely if ever will they entertain the thought, "why are they there?" They are there is about as far as any notice goes. Do they think they have always been there?

Not to give my affliction more gratification that it deserves, I will just say that I am overly curious and to what end? Everything I see, I ask why is that there? It is a habit and the only good or bad thing I can say about my habit, is I am conscious that almost no one is aware of their surroundings and the nature of things. They are living in an un-natural artificial world no different than watching a cartoon with scenery in the background.

In defense of these other people, it makes little difference if they know that they are living above 400 feet of gravel on bedrock and the first layer of bedrock is two thousand feet thick. The mountains over there are a slipped fault line or compression waves.

To complete this topic I will say with all certainty and can prove it, that you can travel the world over and look at the scenery and except for one small location, you will not see anything that has been there forever. What you see is on top of something that was there before. What was there before? Some people give a damn and some don't.

(124) Popular beliefs

In respect to reading or researching information which is in contradiction to existing popular opinion. Good examples of this is that you will not see a Buddhist Monk in a Muslim mosque watching the rituals for the sake of acquiring the knowledge of the Muslim religion, and as well, the Muslims would not allow the Buddhist Monk the opportunity. A Christian or Jew would definitely not go through the experience either, although they are certain it would have no influencing effect on them. Or are they afraid it might? I am sure God would not mind where a Jew or Christian worshipped him, as he is the very same entity being worshipped.

Another classic example is Adolph Hitler and his literary work *Mein Kampf.* Adolph Hitler was one of the best known villains in history and is known worldwide. Adolph Hitler wrote a book wherein he explains his perceptions, beliefs and motivations. If you are to say that you have read Mein Kampf, you are looked at as a skinhead, socialist liberal scumbag, or just some wacko who owns a Ruger and a Doberman Pincer. In fact, everyone should have knowledge of Hitler the person and leader, as well as read Mein Kampf. The reason for this is primarily to be able to identify the next tyrant before he inflicts untold damage to the people of the world. Although there is some risk in this philosophy. If you read Mein Kampf and have knowledge of the history and the time the book was written, one cannot help but understand Hitler's perception of the world at that time. His philosophy on most matters of the world situation was for the most part the common belief in that part of Europe. There are hints in the book, which reflect the possibility of exactly what happened in Germany in following years under his rule. Reading a book of this type by a political hopeful may give a person insight as to what could happen in the future.

Prior to reading Mein Kampf and further study of Hitler, I had a preconceived perception of the man and his philosophy. I perceived him as being a not very intelligent individual, who by hook or crook had surrounding himself with violent bullies and eventually gained control of the German government and its people. I am now of the opinion that Adolph Hitler was far from unintelligent. He had the belief that he could evolve the German nation and its people to a point of grandiose economic stability and power. The basis for Hitler's rise to power was his knowledge of the psychology of speech and persuasion. By the time he had gained control of Germany, he had almost complete approval of the population of Germany. The German people to a great degree had experienced a very bad situation in Germany due to the First World War and a prolonged financial depression. Hitler just amplified the German's feelings and emotions and sold them on *the greatest country in the world* scenario.

The reading of Mein Kampf gives one the thought process of Hitler as well as the reasons for his actions.

It is possible to see his rational, but the end result of all of this was a disaster for Germany and the rest of the world. Hitler had the highest respect for the German people and the Arian race, but in the end he threw them under the bus as his paranoia towards them increased.

I do question if it was possible then or now, for the average citizen to see a disaster on the horizon created by something or someone the majority of the population passionately agrees with. The story of Adolph Hitler, the child loving, dog loving, polite and friendly favorite of the masses, should be known by everyone as a warning of patriotic fervor.

It is fashionable to compare certain individuals to Adolph Hitler. This should not be taken lightly. Hitler was the good the bad and the ugly, and the ugly should not be specified to any other individual without good evidence. Any future American version of Adolph Hitler may not be the obvious, but one who is amplifying what some already believe. Hence he may be undetectable, because all politicians seem to be doing just that.

(125) Individual wealth in the U.S.

Well the next best kept secret in the U.S.----- I just changed my mind, this is the best-kept secret in the U.S.

While on the Internet trying to satisfy my curiosity on another matter, I came across an interesting statistic. This was as much as two years ago, but I doubt if there is a great deal of difference in the numbers. When looking at the first chart or graph, I became more interested in the matter because I found the information hard to believe. I checked other sources, which were all departments of the U.S. Government, and low and behold they verified the first article. What I discovered was that **one in every ten households in America is a millionaire household.**

All of the network sites explained that a millionaire household is any household where the occupants combined worth is over one million dollars. The article did not explain further as to what a household is, but I assume it is a physical structure whether it is a house, apartment or condominium. It was emphasized in all of the documentation that the value of the house hold structure **was not** calculated into household worth. Now this was really interesting to me, as people tend to tie up a great deal of their wealth in their real estate. This being the case, I would have to conclude that a millionaire household has a net worth of a great deal more than a million dollars. Having a household net worth of a million dollars which does not include the value of the structure is much different than one including the structure. If one in ten households are millionaires not counting the structure, just imagine how many there are when counting the structure. I did the research on trying to find out how many millionaires there are in the U.S. and the numbers are staggering. This information may be of little significance to the millionaire households, but it is of great significance to the millions who are struggling financially for such things as rent, food and medicine. I am thinking that there is something wrong with this picture.

Now why all of this is significant, goes back to the perceptions different people have about things and in this case wealth. I am sure if you were to poll residential areas where by necessity people of various degrees of wealth accumulate, asked them how many millionaires there are, you would get a wide range of opinions. Most of us in the U.S. have seen the various households in the cities and rural areas. We are all aware of the difference in the size, age, condition and location of these structures. With some exceptions a person can generally assess the wealth of the people living in these structures. Although these structures vary from shanty to large and ornate, for the purpose of this content we will separate them into upper, middle and lower priced structures which are generally occupied by people in the upper, middle and lower wealth categories.

My opinion is that most lower income people who are born and raised in the lower wealth areas are ill informed as to the vast numbers in the upper category. These people are at best looking to get into the middle category. The middle wealth group is more aware of the wealth categories beneath and above them. They are much more familiar with the lower group as they are slowly infringing into the middle group areas and they are not real happy about this. This is primarily because the lower category people are increasing in numbers and are usually at the center of the town's infrastructure and have no room for expansion other than into the middle category areas. The middle category looks at the fancy houses on the hill and just accepts this as rich people and doesn't give it much more thought than that.

Some of these middle category people live on the fringe of the upper category structures and a few even manage to become upper category people.

What has happened, and for the most part is not planned by the upper category is that the middle category is a big buffer between the lower and upper category. There is little to no social interaction between the upper and lower categories except for domestic labor performed by the lower category for the upper category.

Where am I going with this? For a variety of reasons of which none are very pretty, the lower categories and the upper categories are gaining in numbers while the middle category is diminishing in size.

What is going to happen if this middle category buffer disappears? The increase in numbers of the wealthy category is obviously wealth acquired from the middle and lower groups. There are multitudes of ways this happens, but it does happen. Some of the middle category moves up into the upper category and the remainder are eventually destined to drop to the lower category. You just have to look at our financial system, labor and social system to come to this conclusion.

My perception of this impending situation is that the wealthy category is not giving this problem the attention it deserves. History is full of cases such as this and the repercussions of a two-class system where the upper and the lower category are in direct contact. What happens when people who are struggling find out that there are many millions of people who in their eyes are immensely wealthy? It never worked out well for either group in the past, other than the upper category had a lot more to lose than the lower category.

Giving this matter the consideration it deserves, it appears that the upper category should do everything it can to perpetuate the middle category. This is not good news for the upper category because it requires them to assure the middle category does not slip into the lower category and this will be at the expense of the upper category. Maintaining a middle category requires jobs for these people and preventing them from having to spend all of their wealth on necessary services. The *new money* upper category, which primarily has control of the business sector, has made it into this category doing just the opposite. Downsizing, outsourcing manufacturing and little reinvestment in the U.S. have been some of their tools of profit.

Not being in the upper category and imagining that I am, my thoughts are, do I want to take a little hit now or a potential catastrophic hit in the future?

This scenario may be starting to play out right now, as it is in some other countries. Our current financial and business structure in respect to all three groups appears to be representative of my comments above.

(126) The U.S. financial crisis (2011)

We have a financial crisis going on in this country. It actually started a couple of decades ago, but is only getting attention the last few years. Up until a few years ago the crisis was manageable, so it was not a crisis. To the shock and dismay of the citizens of the U.S. it was brought to their attention that corporations, the private sector in general, oil companies and everyone else on the globe wanted to acquire as much money as they could, regardless of the consequences to our country or its citizens. To make things worse, the very moment these entities weathered the current financial crisis, at the expense of the U.S. citizens and their government, they are kicking us when we are down. I listen to a continuous barrage of news commentary as to who is to blame for our current financial woes. I say that we the citizens are to blame, because we have already forgotten about billions of dollars lost to those who enriched themselves at the expense of others. The unemployment rate stays around 9% and more layoffs are looming in the future. The largest employers in this country are the local, state and the federal governments. Ironically, the private sector is making record profits. How can this be? The unemployment rate increases in direct proportion to the increases in corporate profits? You don't have to be a genius to figure out that the corporations are making more money with fewer employees. That is not the way it is supposed to work and we have been told quite a different story. This story being, the more profits the corporations make, the more they will invest in job producing projects.

Wall Street isn't doing that badly either. My perception of what has and is happening, and it has to be a perception because other people see the same thing I see and have a different opinion, is that the corporations or any of the large employers are producing products at lower labor costs or are outsourcing their production. Another sad aspect of this whole affair is that corporations are paying next to nothing in dividends to their shareholders. In a lot of cases they have taken their profits and bought back their own stock at reduced market rates and low and behold, their stock prices have increased. Now if you are setting on a pile of stock options, this works out very well for you. The price of gasoline at the pump has been such that the oil companies have made billions in profits at the consumer's expense.

Groceries have almost doubled in price and everything else has increased. The private sector is graciously passing on the price increases they are incurring to the citizens. It is pretty obvious that there are a lot of people getting screwed in this whole process. The middle class has their back against the wall as nothing is going right for them. Unless we do something, the middle class will go broke and spend or lose what assets they still have.

To avert a catastrophic national and international crisis, governments initiated stimulus plans to save the banks and corporations as well as stimulus plans for the citizens. This was not a political issue by the Republicans or the Democrats; this was a financial life or death situation. Of course the propaganda machine in this country has had a field day with this issue. At the moment the Democrats are in the hot seat merely because they are in the seat. If the Republicans were in power, they are the ones who would be catching hell for the high unemployment rate and the stimulus money spent.

The Republicans have this brain lock on not raising taxes to the point of fanaticism based upon a false premise. Discussing raising taxes with Republicans is like trying to negotiate with the North Koreans.

The Democrats on the other hand contend that we can borrow and spend our way out of this financial crisis. Of course, that is dependent upon raising taxes. In the short term and at the time of me writing this book, we are days away from either raising the national debt ceiling or not. Both sides are in deadlock negotiations with those who are threatening to not raise the national debt ceiling. Both parties know that if we do not raise the debt ceiling the repercussions will be worse than any financial crisis the world has ever experienced. Assuming that there are no Wackos involved in the whole process, the debt ceiling will be voted on and passed before the deadline regardless of any negotiations. There are two problems with this scenario. The first being that the closer we get to the deadline the less confidence there is in U.S. treasury notes worldwide. If we get too close to the deadline or we have a Presidential candidate state that they would not raise the debt ceiling, the more damage there is going to be inflicted on the world stock markets, even though the debt ceiling will inevitably be raised. More dangerous than that, is the possibility of a single Wacko congressman at the last minute obstructing the passage of the legislation. Currently there are several Wackos in Congress capable of such an act of stupidity. That is why the vote cannot be at the last minute.

It was a stupid error putting such controversial issues up for vote with the legislation to increase the national debt. The citizens of the U.S. are being held hostage by the same people they elected to protect them.

My perception of the issues involved which drive us to the brink, are that the issues are as much philosophical as they are practical. On one side you have the traditional Republican Party which is being sidetracked by some of their own constituency. The traditional more experienced Republican Party cannot gain control of the government without their cooperation and they know it. It's the tail wagging the dog scenario. The Republican Party being Conservative in beliefs are of the position that there should be no increases in taxes and U.S. government spending should be cut to solve the national debt problem and the government should be reduced in size. (Which I will address later). Amazingly enough, they have spending cut proposals which the majority of Americans oppose, to solve the problem. Somehow by not increasing tax revenue, which would surely fall on the rich, there will be a miraculous increase in job production. If we are in the shitter right now, at the current levels of taxation, how could maintaining this level possibly have any effect on job creation?

If the theory had any validity at all, it would require an additional major tax reduction for wealthy individuals or corporations for this to work. This means less revenue and higher national debt and this would require more drastic spending cuts to all programs funded by the government. Any additional cuts to reduce the national debt would be at the loss of jobs, which in fact are a source of revenue for the government, and further exasperates the problem. A good part of the Republican policy or plan is that the wealthy individuals or corporations will use the money they are not paying in taxes and invest in enterprises which will create thousands of new jobs and get this country back on its feet. Well, nothing could be further from the truth. Right now the private sector is setting on two to three trillion dollars of reserves and they are not using any of it for that purpose. Is another trillion thrown into the pot going to make a difference? I am sure it won't. Oh sure, the wealthy have to do something with their money, they can't have it setting around in boxcars. The wealthy at this point are not out there looking for a way to make money in any way which would require a labor force; they are just trying not to lose what they already have. Every conceivable method for retaining their wealth is being utilized.

Of course there are billions being made on commodities and the markets, but this is just shifting the money around which does nothing for the job market. Gold goes to

$1700.00 per ounce and silver to $35.00 per ounce. Billions have been made and billions are tied up in these commodities which are doing nothing for our national economy. My perception of the Republican plan is that it will not work and in the last twenty years hasn't worked.

Now for the brain locked red faced Republicans who have thrown this book in the garbage, I will afford the Democrats the same opportunity. My perception of the Democratic philosophy is that they have a whole lot more poor constituents in their ranks than the Republicans. Whereas the wealthy do not require a great deal in social assistance to survive, the lower categories do. This being the case, their philosophy as to what is required to run this country is entirely different. Their philosophy is that every citizen should be in the middle class or have every opportunity with social assistance of achieving this. This would probably require the redistribution of the wealth of all individuals within the U.S. by taxation. The middle class cannot support the lower class or they would also slip into the lower class. Therefore the upper class will have to cough up the lion's share of the wealth required. Their philosophy is that if the upper class invests in the middle and lower classes, they will eventually get their money back in profits. There are several flaws in this scenario. You can spend the revenue you think the wealthy class is going to be taxed, but in reality the wealthy for the most part do not pay that much in taxes. You don't tax accrued wealth, you tax income profits. Net profit is a funny thing. Corporations like General Electric can have billions of dollars in profits and their net taxable income will be $0.00. Then you have the issue of raising taxes on business and corporations from 35% to 39% and they just pass the proposed profit loss on to the consumer. Hence the middle and lower class can pay the taxes for the wealthy. Now how is that going to work? We are already paying the taxes and the oil spill problems of the oil companies at the pump. That would be just a taste of the same medicine. I guess we will just continue borrowing money to finance the American society.

My perception is that the Democratic philosophy will not work either. Not to say that both philosophies do not have some good ideas, but when they are polarized, it is of no consequence.

I would just like to insert at this point that if you join any group, whether it be the Democratic party, the Republican party, a union, a church denomination, a club, a society, an organization or any other entity, you have obligated yourself to them and you have lost a certain amount of free thought and speech. You are subject to peer pressure and individuals who will take advantage of your presence. That is the social order of things. By the same token, history has taught us that pure socialism, capitalism and all the other pure form of *ism,s* do not work. It is taking the best qualities of each and utilizing them that is the most effective.

I am sure everyone has a different perception of what will work to stabilize the U.S. economy in the short and long term and everyone's perception will be opposed by the existing philosophies. I have my own opinion as to what will work and it has little to do with politics. The observations that I have addressed and the way I perceive them have led me to a conclusion. (How conclusions are arrived at I will also address later).

(127) Solving our financial crisis in months not decades

My conclusion is that the goal of the U.S. government should be to have lower taxes, have social benefits, have available jobs, have no national debt, have an acceptable quality of life for the lower wealth group, a large middle wealth group as well as have a wealthy group.

Well how can you obtain all of this, which should satisfy everyone?

Protectionism is a function of a government who has restrictions or tariffs on trade imports and exports. The free will of citizens to import or export and purchase what they desire on the free world market is not protectionism. Every person on the Earth does this every day. The primary reason that the U.S. is in the financial situation it is in today is due to the choices we make when purchasing materials, commodities and all other items.

Our industrial manufacturing base in this country has collapsed due to the choices the citizens have made. The private sector that we have which sells goods, is essentially pimping for foreign industries and foreign labor.

The private sector and the citizens of the U.S. have to make hard choices of selectively purchasing goods that are manufactured within the United States. Why the choice would initially be difficult is because we are not manufacturing the full scale of goods we consume. Trust me, if there is a demand for something, someone will quickly make it available. Of course this would require constructing a manufacturing base and would take hundreds of thousands of workers. That *scared* money that has been sitting on the sidelines and the people who own it are just crazy to invest it in a sure thing. The initial struggle for the consumer is that the cost of goods would be considerably higher until production is in full swing. I think most Americans would pay more for what they actually need and have a lot less junk lying around, for the sake of this country's financial security.

The U.S. auto makers alone are up to the challenge of increasing production and it would have a significant affect on the economy. If this rebuilding of the manufacturing base requires loans or loan guarantees by the government, so be it.

As to essential products, we have the agricultural production to satisfy our needs, so basically our shortcoming is our energy requirements. We have the energy resources, but we have screwed ourselves in this arena. We will have to do what we should have been doing for the last fifty years, which is to develop these resources. There are commodities that we have to import and there is absolutely nothing wrong with importing what is required and in turn, we can export what other countries require. But the bottom line is; if it is not manufactured in the U.S. don't purchase it unless you have to. It may be quite a step down for some, but I think they should be able to survive with a Cadillac or Lincoln. You can bet that whatever you want a product to do or to look like, someone in the U.S. will produce it.

Of course U.S. companies who have moved abroad or are having auto parts and appliances manufactured in foreign countries will have to move back to the U.S. This may not be to their liking, but I think the U.S. consumer can live with that resentment.

I believe that U.S. citizens will accept a policy whereby we sell oil and gas leases to U.S. based oil companies for domestic consumption, even though their bid is a little lower on the royalties. I would have little problem with government loans to them and I am sure there would be a market on Wall Street for their issued stocks considering the profits in petroleum.

This turnaround might be to the dismay of other countries, but it being a choice of American consumers to buy American goods it is reasonable and not a national conspiracy to harm them, I think they will have to accept this. There are many countries who do not like anything with *Made in the U.S.A.* marked on it and they are making a choice not to purchase these products.

I perceive that this decision made by the citizens of the U.S. would turn our economy around in the very short term. I also perceive that if this decision is not made by the American public, we are committing financial suicide. We cannot keep borrowing money from countries and at the same time spend the money purchasing their products. We cannot continue to give money to social programs that are purchasing foreign goods. We cannot continue to give our fossil fuel resources to corporations, whether foreign or domestic, who receive subsidies, tax benefits, and make huge profits.

The citizens of the U.S. currently just pay the price for petroleum products, whine a lot and do little else. We are at the mercy of big oil corporations because they are the only entities in place who have the technology and available equipment to recover petroleum products, and for God's sake we don't want to have the socialistic stigma of competing with foreign companies that are controlling our natural resources.

They are sitting with their hand on the spicket and have the ability to raise or lower the price of petroleum products as they see fit and appear to do that when any newsworthy event happens, whether it involves oil or not.

Our government or the citizens should receive a reasonable share of the profit from our natural resources, whether it is by eliminating subsidies or by taxation. It is obvious that BIG OIL has a large following in our Congress. If that were not the case, these oil companies would not be receiving subsidies and tax breaks while they are making record profits.

My perception of an American economy where domestic products are purchased and millions of jobs created will save our butt, but it will do little good if someone shuts off the petroleum spicket. We have the resources and ability to become self-sufficient, but we cannot do this unless U.S. citizens and Congress pursues that goal.

(128) Televangelists

My perception of televangelism is a very negative one. If the reader's perception is a positive one, they can just skip to the next topic or hang in there and read about mine. Which is; Televangelism for the most part has depleted the finances of thousands of Americans in the name of the Lord. Hundreds of millions of dollars have been received by these people in the name of the Lord and I don't think the Lord got a fair shake in almost every case. The history of televangelists is full of instances where they broke the law, were involved in less than moral conduct, acquired and spent vast fortunes on themselves, and the list goes on. Those who have not been documented of this behavior are at least suspected of it. There may be exceptions to the rule such as Billy Graham, but who is to say people involved with him did not take advantage of the situation. The public perception, by many, is that televangelists are spreading the word of God. In reality they are raising money so that they can spread the word of God. They're primary purpose being to raise money.

I am familiar with all of them and have watched their programs out of curiosity. In almost every case, I do not like what I see. I see propaganda, fraud, misuse of funds, preying on people, hypnotism, self-righteousness and questionable business practices. All in the name of God and no taxes.

For someone who sees through the facade, the antics and rhetoric are ridiculous. These people have no reservations about asking others for their money regardless of their financial status, even if they have to borrow it. They even suggest that you bequeath your assets to them when you die. On one hand they are doing this for God, and on the other hand they are living lavish life styles. As the money raised is supposed to be for the spreading of the gospels, this appears to be out and out fraud to me. Jim Baker went to prison for his actions and I have a lot of sympathy for him and Tammy. Not for what they had done, but because they had been manipulated constantly by others in the televangelist organization who were guilty of the same thing. This being fraud and taking money under false pretenses, and they got away with it and continue to get away with it.

The donors, because of their beliefs have few options but to donate due to their obligations to the Lord, because that is just what they are told. It is all just *seed money* anyway and will be returned tenfold. There are a lot of sincere religious leaders out there who are administering and teaching the gospel and who do not live in multimillion-dollar estates. I am inclined to donate my money to one of these leaders. I think your dollar will go a lot further, as your televangelist dollar went for a $300.00 sink faucet and I am not so sure the Lord is all that interested in sink faucets.

The troubling aspect of this situation is that for the most part the televangelists are Christians who can mentally justify their actions by interpretation of the scriptures. In their own mind they are guilty of nothing either legally or morally, or in the eyes of the Lord. I perceive televangelism as a shameful practice as it is being performed, but it would not have to be that way. Do they do any good at all? Yes. The same as a charity who gives 10% of their income to starving children in Ethiopia. 10% is better than nothing and I guess that is a good thing, but it could be 80% of a better thing.

(129) The Earth

I cannot say for certain how the Earth was formed, why it is the size it is, why it rotates in twenty-four hours and many other things about it. What I do know about the Earth is what has been scientifically substantiated and what I have seen of it.

Some Fundamental Creationists do not agree with proven scientific facts which have been accepted as facts by the general public. Centuries ago, most of the information that was available about the Earth was explained by the religious community and scientific evidence had to work around that. It is now somewhat different in that scientific facts for the most part are accepted and religious teachings have to work around these. Not to say the two are incompatible, but it requires some rethinking and new religious interpretation.

I know why the Earth is round; because it has to be. All celestial bodies are round, as they have to be round also. They are compelled to be round due to the force of gravity. There are a few or I should say billions of exceptions to being round and these are all small objects with gravitational force less than is required to pull them into a round configuration. All of this brings up an interesting topic. When God created the universe, did he have to comply with the laws of physics or did he create the laws of physics at the same time?

The Earth has a molten iron core with progressively lighter molten materials outside that core and then a thin crust of hardened lighter material, except where in rare places the heavier elements were forced into the crust. The surface of the earth seems rough to us, but in reality it is smooth, as the continent's elevations are negligible as compared to the diameter of the Earth.

The Earth is very old and its age has been estimated at around 4 billion years. Old enough that almost the entire original crust has been replaced many times by molten material from beneath. For Creationists, this is not exactly as described in Genesis, but then again, creating the Universe was probably more complicated than a single paragraph, and maybe the details are not any of our concern.

The Earth definitely has living organisms on it and there were living organisms here a billion years ago. Whether or not these were the genetic ancestors of our living organisms today, I cannot say. Although some are quite similar.

There were definitely dinosaurs on earth *before* there were humans, regardless of what Sarah Palin believes. Before and after the dinosaurs there were a multitude of other creatures, which with few exceptions were different than we have today. Whether these evolved into what we have today, they were modified or replaced, I can also not say. In the recent past 100,000 years or so, there were creatures which appeared to be primates. Sometime later, there was what is referred to as modern man. Whether these evolved from other primates or put here I cannot say. Creationist theology aside, humans have changed to adapt to their environment. People have definitely gotten taller.

How the events described in Genesis took place I cannot say, but they started around four billion years ago and may have taken place during the entire history of the Earth or the later part of it.

(130) What they didn't tell you

I am surprised at how little Americans know about U.S. history and as well I am surprised at how little I have known about it throughout my life. There are two reasons for this, the first being, it was not taught and it was not available to read, and the other is that nobody cares.

With the advent of the internet and access to historic documents, a whole new history is revealed. I know I have addressed this before, but in order to delete a topic along the lines of "You can't handle the truth," I just added this in its place.

(131) Well I am tired of this, how about you?

In finishing this book, I would like to explain something. Most of the content of this book appears to be negative in nature. This is not because I or other people are negative minded individuals who spend a lot of time thinking about people. I am a places and things person. My interests are varied, but I have an interest in public policy regardless of who is making the policy. I believe that the U.S. is a Democratic Republic and believe that people should have respect for this. Some people who are claiming patriotism have less respect for the institution than I do or they would be satisfied with it or change it in an honorable manner described in the Constitution of the United States.

THE END